PROPS FOR UNDER MY SKIN

"Whether you are covered in tattoos or don't have a single piece of ink, *Under My Skin* is a badass read. Drew's unique tools to help sharpen resilience, mental fortitude, and overcome personal tragedy and grief are told in a fresh and inspiring way. His ability to laugh when others might cry and to poke fun at himself had me laughing out loud throughout the book."

—**CLINT EMERSON**, retired Navy Seal, *New York Times* bestselling author
@100deadlyskills

"Man…this book speaks to me. Every time Drew tells us to 'always be writing our own comeback story,' it reminds me of my life. I wish I had this book all those years I was scrapping just to put food on the table, trying to break into the country music industry. And I love the vulnerable, human way the book uses Drew's specific tattoos to cover so [many] topics everyone will benefit from."

—**ELVIE SHANE**, country music singer
@elvieshanemusic

"I've known Drew for years: I've been on his podcast, and we recently got tattoos together. But I had no idea what to expect from this book. *Under My Skin* goes DEEP. I got chills following Drew's decades-long tattoo journey, which he uses to communicate his greatest triumphs and tragedies in a way that is both personally raw and extremely motivating. His communication style is piss-in-your-pants funny — especially because it's who he really is."

—**BOB MARIER**, sober coach
@sober_coach

"*Under My Skin* is a hilarious, emotional, and inspiring book. Drew is the definition of authentic. What you see is 100% what you get! His journey has been a thrill to watch and very motivational."

— **JOSH ALTMAN**, Million Dollar Listing real estate agent
@thejoshaltman

"As a professional race car driver in NASCAR, I know what it's like to be the underdog. *Under My Skin* will inspire every underdog who knows backwards is never an option!"

— **SPENCER BOYD**, NASCAR driver
@spencerboydpr

UNDER MY SKIN

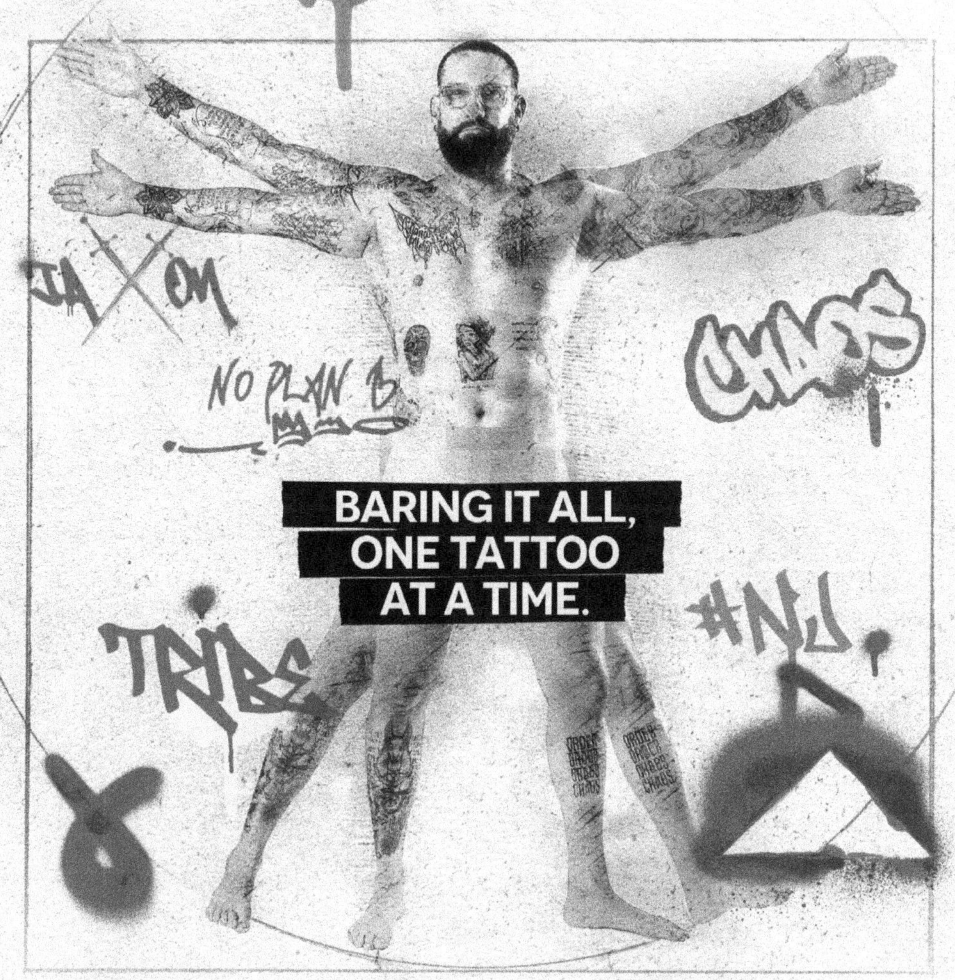

BY DREW PLOTKIN
(AKA THE DERM DUDE™)

DERM DUDE

Under My Skin
Copyright ©2022 by Muuaa Inc.

Published by
Muuaa Inc.

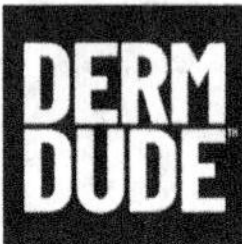

Hardcover ISBN: 979-8-9868329-0-6
Paperback ISBN: 979-8-9868329-1-3
eISBN: 979-8-9868329-2-0

For Dad —
Heaven has no traffic jams. The food always comes out fast.
And the NFL Sunday Ticket never goes up in price.

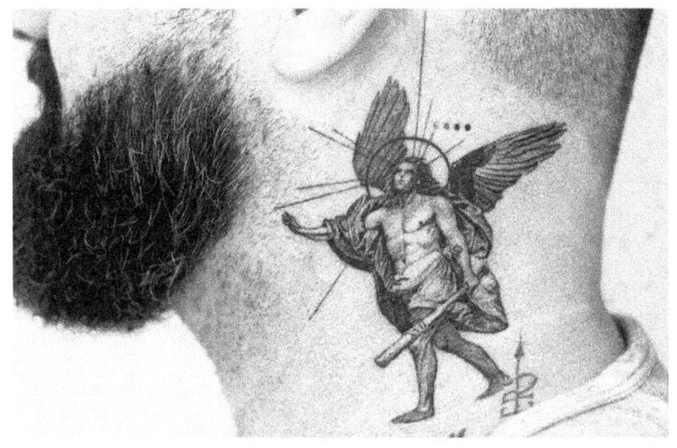

@oscarakermo

And to Zoe, Jaxon, Harper, and Ayana —
Time flies. Every moment with you is my greatest joy.

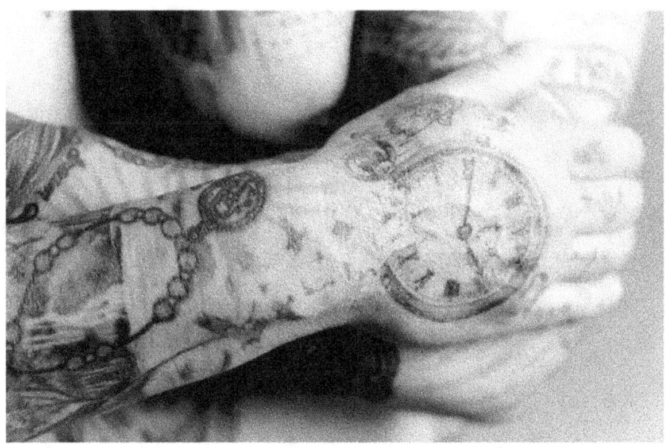

@turan.nyc

CONTENTS

INTRODUCTION

MY BODY,
THE GIANT POST-IT® NOTE

I love tattoos.

I also hate them.

That seems to shock people. But since I'm covered in them — arms, chest, hands, fingers, ribs, and torso, my neck is fairly full, I even have tattoos on my head and ear — so you can guess which side usually wins.

People collect things. Some collect coins, stamps, baseball cards, and even cars.

I collect…tattoos.

To date, my collection has cost me somewhere in the range of about $125,000. And I definitely have more open tattoo "real estate" I plan to occupy.

Tattoos have unintentionally become my pathway to constant change — which is ironic, given their permanence. Irreversibly changing my body with each tattoo has always been a huge adrenaline rush for me. The concept of "forever" and "no turning back" gets my heart pumping, and I experience an out-of-body high when the needle touches me for the first time. A sizzle of electricity runs through me; I know shit just got real, and I walk away…forever different than when I awoke that day. To be clear, I don't get off on the pain of tattoos. I hate the pain, so if you're looking for a pain fetish type of book, this ain't it (no judgment, dude). It's also not a book about how to score tattoo appointments with A-list celebrity ink artists with millions of Instagram stalkers. This is a book about using that surface ink to go deeper. Much, much deeper.

Some people study philosophy, and while I've slowly stumbled through books by a few great minds and inquisitive thinkers, like Viktor Frankl and Sun Tzu, I've always had an inexplicable thirst to etch out my own guiding philosophies. I suppose it's my way of reminding myself what I'm capable of and the type of human being I want to be. That might sound like some sort of bullshitzo babble I came up with while tripping on mushrooms. Nope.

My philosophical guideposts emerge most clearly through life experience.

The majority of my adult life has been spent building brands that sell beauty and personal care products to the masses: Weight-loss systems, workout devices, skin and hair care products, hair loss prevention and restoration and cosmetics. The company I built helped my clients sell well over $1 billion in products and services for countless worldwide brands via the creative marketing, infomercials, TV spots, and social media campaigns that my agency created. I also directed some of the top names in the biz — JLO, Cindy Crawford, Paris Hilton, Serena Williams, Drew Brees, Bruce Jenner (pre-Caitlyn), various *Shark Tank* cast members, along with a who's who list of Olympians, TV doctors, and fitness gurus like Jillian Michaels, Tony Horton, and many more.

Whenever the economy shifted and someone asked me, "How's business?" I often jokingly (but truthfully) replied that as long as people were fat, bald, and wrinkly, I could make money. And I did. Internally, though, I was often conflicted about making a living by selling products and services to people looking to "fix" themselves. My compromise was to religiously avoid the phony sales gimmicks and bait-and-switch tactics commonly deployed in the direct marketing world. Instead, I put an emphasis on the human stories that showcased the positive impact our products and brands had on people's lives. And even though I didn't personally make billions, I made enough to create a stable, happy home for my family.

So while I professionally lived in the world of quick cosmetic fixes, my tattoos have never been a fix for anything. If you think that Sanskrit symbol about the virtues of patience tattooed on your torso is some kind of quick fix for your road rage issues, you'll be sorely disappointed while driving home in rush hour traffic later. Don't get me wrong: Tattoos can be a uniquely life-changing experience. I'm just saying there's no such thing as "magic ink" to instantly change reality.

But when I do find myself drowning in a sea of dark clouds, heading deeper into a shitstorm of a 100% certified pissed-off kind of mood, a simple glance at almost any ink-covered part of my body calms me and reminds me of my purpose. That may sound simplistic, but my tattoos commemorate events, milestones, celebrations, heartbreaks, and everything in between. They help motivate me, they mark my time and my very existence, while serving as visual reminders of my own "WHY?" — and they are absolutely, without fail, my own personal life "cheat sheet." They're my on-call therapist to keep me in the right mindset and reinforce my core beliefs — not just for that moment when the needle penetrates my flesh, but forever.

What's imprinted *on* my skin is my closest understanding of what's actually *under* my skin.

Admittedly, sometimes my tattoos are a social crutch, giving me an excuse not to express myself directly in person. In my mind, I'm already visually sharing my story with you, but like all stories, the ones I wear on my skin are open to interpretation, and how they are told evolves with the passing of time. (When strangers regularly ask me, "Why do you have so many tattoos?" I usually say, "So I have something to read in line at Starbucks." So I guess, in reality, I'm only partially joking.)

Making my body into an autobiographical philosophy textbook was more accidental than by design. Starting when I was twenty years old, I began my tattoo collection slowly, little by little. Some people set out to complete a full arm sleeve or cover their entire bodies, accomplishing those goals in less time than it took me to summon the balls for my first one. That just wasn't me. I didn't have the foresight or "ink-spiration" out of the gate to flip the switch from unmarked virgin skin to full-body ink overnight. I crawled my way into this oversized human canvas of mine over the course of thirty years of human experiences and events I felt drawn to immortalize.

Many of my tattoos started small and grew or morphed over time, merging and commingling across my body, forming new, unplanned channels of connection. As a result, I can't and won't count my tattoos. They don't operate in isolation any more than my organs do. They're a singular elaborate system that makes the invisible parts of my life visible — to others, yes, but most importantly, to me.

So while I don't have an exact tattoo tally, here's how a math moron like me breaks down the numbers: The average tattoo machine moves the needle up and down between 50 and 3,000 times per minute. Which means that, given the surface area I've covered over the last thirty years, it's safe to say I've been poked and zapped millions of times over by now. (I've known a lot of assholes in my lifetime, but I've literally been touched by millions of pricks.)

Some people envision their tattoos as creative masterpieces, making them a walking work of art. But my body is more sketch pad than master plan. It's an imperfect mashup of experiences, ideas, philosophies, dreams, fears, aspirations, and impossible-to-ignore Post-it notes to myself. They're reminders of where I've been, where I'm at, and where I do and don't want to go. And most importantly, they're permanent.

Talk to someone after getting their first tattoo, and they have one of two reactions: They either regret it and will never get another, or they are instantly addicted, their mind racing with thoughts of "What should I get next — and how soon can I get it?" Decades after my first tattoo (which, honestly, should've left me with nothing but regret), it was that "What's next?" instinct that brought me to Bali.

In 2019, I traveled halfway around the world to Bali for a rare three-day tattoo experience with Balaz, a highly sought-after (and elusive) artist who is extremely selective about who and what he will tattoo. (Damn creative geniuses.) Balaz is one whacky, moody MOFO. Originally from Hungary, I met him in NYC at Bang Bang Tattoo, a true tattoo mecca. Balaz's style is single-needle, forming fine black and gray lines to create symbolism that connects with the sacred and the ancient, often implementing a talisman — an object able to protect or heal — into the imagery. I wanted to add a new tattoo based on a particularly heart-wrenching recent life event, so I was willing to travel great lengths to work with the right artist for this piece — and I knew Balaz was it.

Given his esoteric and outright trippy style, I guess it's no surprise that he chose to spend our first full day together NOT tattooing or sketching or designing. Instead, we talked. Specifically, about the philosophy of tattoos, and not just the tattoo we would create in the coming days, but ALL of my tattoos, existing and future. *What story was I telling? What did I hope to communicate?* Going far beyond tattoos, we talked and waded into topics like life and death and the full spectrum of life's experiences: joy and sadness, fears and failures, victories and dreams. It was like tattoo church, with tequila.

For a moment, I forgot I was in Bali for a tattoo — versus a transformational retreat for my wounded spirit and soul. That trip took me on a journey where no plane could carry me. It was the allure of a new kick-ass tattoo that brought me there, but the mental, emotional, and spiritual workover I experienced makes a colonoscopy feel like a pat on the back. Getting a tattoo is never comfortable or enjoyable (and anyone who says hours of flesh-piercing needle punctures feels good has issues), but this one stung in ways I couldn't have imagined, dragging up life traumas and embedding upon my chest a path toward acceptance, forgiveness, and even some inner peace and healing.

That night, staring at all of my existing tattoos reflecting back at me in a rain-splattered Balinese window, I no longer thought of all the designs individually. I knew in that instance that while they were each tattooed on me as a singular expression, across decades of time, they had joined forces to form a larger work-in-progress, an open exhibition of my ever-unfolding story.

For the first time, I wasn't seeing specific tattoos; I saw the entirety of my living canvas with clear eyes — the enigmatic symbols, imperfect shapes, and words and phrases in languages I don't even speak. There it was, staring back at me: My history, my future, and everything in between. It was anything but calculated, but I'd inadvertently created my own personal road map. These were my notes, and my body was my guide. It was my source for finally understanding...*ME*.

As my skin transformed over the decades, so did my life.

Years before my first tattoo, at age sixteen, I became the youngest journalist ever permitted on death row to conduct an in-person interview with a death row inmate. That might have been a clue that I was teeing-up a rather unconventional life.

After college, I received an Emmy nomination as a TV news producer (a time that led to a series of epic fuck-ups and significant tattoos). Then, starting with an accidental entry into the infomercial business, I went on to launch the ad agency that made me a sought-after name, directing and producing content for an endless stream of high (and low) profile products and brands. And along the way, I co-founded a non-profit that delivered thousands of free, complex rehabilitation wheelchairs to severely disabled kids in developing countries, many of whom lived mostly on the ground prior to receiving the gift of mobility.

That is all a world away from where I started, in the dysfunctional family trenches of New Jersey. We're either victims or survivors. I believe this to my core, as much as it often pisses some people off when I say it. Shit beyond our control happens to all of us. What makes you a victim or a survivor is not what happens to you, but what you do with the reality of it moving forward.

That's why I'm always writing my comeback story. Many of my tattoos are sparked by events that challenged my will to continue and nearly derailed me. From suicides and near-death experiences of those close to me, to my own personal failures, these events threatened to make me a victim rather than a survivor. But it's not a comeback story if you don't journey far and deep. When I experience a setback, fresh ink is my way of taking back control and rewriting my ever-evolving redemption story.

Wearing your life on your skin does tend to attract attention. I'm a big guy at 6'4, 240 pounds, so whenever possible, I upgrade to more comfortable seats on planes. Inevitably, I'll catch someone across the aisle snapping a photo. One older woman recently said, "Are you somebody? I know you are! Can I take a picture to send it to my nephew? He'll know who you are." I might not be the "somebody" they have in mind, but in those moments, I remind myself. "Yeah, I *am* somebody." So why bother to correct them? (I was relieved when *Game Of Thrones* finally ended so I could stop fielding questions about when I'd be back as Drogo…)

The attention is not always favorable or flattering, however. I'm either "somebody" or the WRONG kind of somebody. For every person who asks for a selfie, another pulls away from me. I've observed women sliding their purses to the opposite side of me or clutching their bags tighter as I walk past. Others stare on flights when I open the overhead bin, afraid I will steal something. Even my own neighbors in an upscale beach community have mistaken me for a maintenance guy, asking me to do odd jobs for them when they see me walking…to my own house on the beach.

Though, admittedly, I do like to fuck with these assumptions at times. Recently, I was in Vegas for the biggest fight of the year. Ringside tickets went for upwards of $25k — if you could even get them. We were in the baller crowd, with Magic Johnson, Steve Harvey, and Rick Ross and his blinding bling next to me. My buddy — who'd flown there on his private jet — realized he didn't have a ticket for his pilot. So, already dressed for the part in a black button down, boots, and tinted shades, I walked outside the arena to assume my role of 'Fake Personal Bodyguard'. Strategically positioned in sight of the ticketing and (legitimate) security area, with the pilot next to me, I kept one finger in my ear and another discreetly speaking into my hand (i.e., imaginary security communication), then swiftly ushered him inside — past multiple ticket counters and various security checkpoints, right to ringside.

To the average person, the fact that I wanted to be invisible my entire life, only to become impossible to miss, seems like a contradiction. But it was an evolution. By my 40s, I had become something I hadn't planned and wouldn't have recognized when I got my first tattoo twenty years prior. I wasn't asking myself, *What will people think? Will they want to take my picture or move away from me?* It was far more instinctual and organic than it was strategic. I gradually morphed from a big guy, not always comfortable in my own skin and looking to hide, into someone completely and forever incapable of blending in. If I wanted to keep writing my story on my terms, I needed to be brutally honest…with myself. So I placed the value of permanent visual truths over my desire to go unnoticed or disappear.

Certain tattoos are easier to hide than others. My first hand tattoo was a huge milestone that demanded serious practical considerations. It was a ripping-the-cord type of decision that meant I could never give up on my personal dreams and settle for a "normal" corporate job. I was my own boss — for life. A similar feeling emerged when the needle first touched my neck. I wasn't just committing to that design *but an entire lifestyle*. It was my way of telling the rest of the "conforming" world to GO FUCK YOURSELF.

While my body tells a story I design, I am not always the hero of this story. The reality is, I fall down a lot. But I also have an insatiable willingness to get back up. My tattoos make no effort to hide or gloss over these stumbles. By imprinting this journey on my body, I hold myself accountable. I'm forced to physically confront my internal reality daily, the inescapable truth of who I am. Tattoos are my time machine back to the past. They keep me committed to perpetually learning and growing from past events and feelings. They remind me of moments too easily lost and forgotten with the passage of time.

If I forget where I am or lose my way, any mirror or recent photo has the guidance I need. My tattooed body is the lighthouse that anchors my reality and reminds me where I'm at in this stage of my journey. Human beings love to rewrite history, especially our own. Tattoos protect me against the revisionist history with which I might otherwise be tempted to bullshit myself. Yes, I've conceived and curated each design, but I approach each new tattoo with a critical sense of unchangeable truthfulness. No rewrites, no whiteout, no do-overs. I'm marked by my past…my truth — for life.

These ink-stained hieroglyphics also guide me toward the future. They're the beliefs and values I aspire to uphold, the life I hope to lead: where to go, what to avoid and who to be.

That's why my tattoos don't just animate my inspiration and help me manifest my dreams, but they also drive me to be the father I want to be for my four miracle kids and the person I want to be in the world. No, my tattoos don't give me superpowers, but they have helped shape me and built the mindset I credit with getting me this far. They memorialize the life events I've both willingly and really-fucking-unwillingly experienced, a constant reminder I can never fully outrun them. Or myself and my own angels and demons. They solidify and validate the path I've chosen, victories, missteps, and all.

Many of my tattoo designs I contemplated for years, laboring over rounds of revisions and carefully selecting the artist. A few are just simple text or the work of an inexperienced artist — or, in one case, a half-drunken afterthought. But every one of my tattoos is significant to me. Every marking matters.

For better or worse, they ain't pumping out more Drew anytime soon, so my unused remaining surface area is prime real estate. And since human skin starts to sag and crepe over time, some tattoo styles become a challenge after a certain age. But for now, as I turn the page on 50 years, there's ample space and firm enough skin to keep the ink flowing. More artists to discover, more innovative technology to try, and most importantly, more stories to tell that will bring me back to the tattoo chair. When I look at my remaining tattoo-free skin, I contemplate what lies ahead, what changes I'll endure, and what comebacks I'm yet to write — inch by fleshy inch.

VIRGIN INK
SHEDDING A TEAR FOR THE SHITTIEST TATTOO

Sometime around my third year at Arizona State, I went to a Grateful Dead show. I wasn't a Deadhead and didn't even know much of their music, but it was a party with no shortage of booze and other ingestibles that fulfilled my primary life's mission back then, which was being mindless and surrounded by attractive females. On that particular night, I exceeded even my own idiotic standards, combining large cups of Jack Daniels with acid and ecstasy (or whatever it was that we scooped up tailgating in the parking lot). I'd also just come off a few days with no sleep, because I'd recently discovered other sleep-depriving recreational activities — so my body was more than a little compromised.

Mid-concert, I had a strange sense that something wasn't right. I vividly remember losing my balance, wobbling, and falling forward into a full faceplant. While being wheeled out on a stretcher, I was just alert enough to see thousands of tie-dyed concert-goers tripping out to Dead tunes, blissed out and oblivious with their plastic beer cups firmly in hand. My eyes closed and I completely 10,000% left my body. No bullshit. I floated off the stretcher, up into the sky, watching my body being wheeled into the ambulance. Parts of my life appeared with crystal clarity, like my mother's voice as she practiced reading with me when I was in the first grade. As I looked down at my body and fought to get back into it, I was overwhelmed by the guilt and shame of what my death would bring. What a pathetic way to leave the world.

By the time I managed to "re-enter" my body, I opened my eyes to see I was alone in a hospital room, with God-knows-what being pumped into me via multiple tubes. I ripped everything out, grabbed my clothes, raced out of the hospital, and snagged a cab home. No doubt, the severe dehydration, mixed with sleep deprivation and a hefty dose of hallucinogens played some wild tricks on my brain. And yet, the visions and sensations I felt that day were entirely real. My body was calling it quits, and either by biological luck or sheer will, I was getting a second chance.

Of course I was still too dumb to see it as another chance at the time, so a few days later I headed to Mexico for Spring Break. The party raged around me, but nothing felt normal for me anymore. Music, beer, girls — it was all like nails on a chalkboard. Everything inside me was broken. I wanted to be ANYWHERE but there. So without telling anyone, I went to the airport and flew home. I just needed to be gone. And I was. I needed some type of direction. Some meaning. A goal. Or I would go off a cliff — if I hadn't already.

Like many twenty-year-olds, I was lost. After making my way from New Jersey to Arizona State, I mistakenly thought joining a fraternity, all-night keg parties, and waking up "wherever with whomever" was my path to discovering who I was. Turns out, it couldn't have been more wrong.

Assimilating into college meant undoing the Drew I'd become in high school. When I graduated from high school in New Jersey, I finally felt comfortable in my own skin. But that was a long and rocky road. Growing up, I often felt out of place or in the way, including always being the tallest kid in my class growing up — an attribute that, off of a basketball court, doesn't always reward you until later in life. My skin was also *covered* in acne. Being different as a teenager, whatever that looks like, is undesirable. When you're uncomfortable in your own skin, fitting in is an impossibility. I wanted to hide and disappear, but my clumsy physicality and inability to pick up social cues left me insecure and feeling empty inside.

I straddled social groups with equal gawkiness. I connected with the jocks, theater kids, rockers, and AV club equally, but none of them singularly fit me. And in high school, if you don't fit somewhere, it's easy to feel like nobody.

If the home environment you grow up in helps shape you, it makes sense that I was bent, crooked, and off-angle in many ways. My father was the simplest and most complicated person rolled into one. Fiercely loyal and unapologetically short-tempered, you could always feel his presence when he walked into a room. Whether he was knocking someone out cold at a casino table in Atlantic City or throwing punches on an airplane on a family flight to Las Vegas for Thanksgiving, if you pushed his buttons, he was gonna light up. (In fairness, both of those individuals referenced above got what they deserved.) He particularly hated excuses, especially an "If...then" argument. One day, I used the forbidden "if" word, and he looked at me squarely and said, "IF my grandmother had balls, she would be my grandfather. Don't ever use the word IF around me again. It's an excuse and a loser word." He was equally uncharitable toward unearned rewards. When some of my friends received gifts for our eighth-grade graduation, I made the mistake of asking my father for the same. "You want a reward? For finishing eighth-grade? You want me to thank YOU because you go to school versus cleaning toilets or sweeping streets all day? When you graduate medical school or law school or any school that shows you are on your way to a career (that's legal), I'll gladly get you a gift." His dry, sarcastic delivery made it hard to distinguish between a joke and a threat. Like that time at the Apple Store when he wanted to ask a question and an Apple employee wearing a branded "Genius" shirt told him, "Uh, it will be at least 45 minutes to speak with a Genius." My father instantly replied, "Oh yeah? How long to speak with an ASSHOLE?" And he walked out of the store.

On the one hand, he was my absolute hero and role model, with many admirable qualities. But he was also a human pressure cooker, and his temperamental nature was a constant reality in my childhood.

At thirteen, I walked in on him trying to kill himself. My mother and I followed his ambulance to the hospital, and when I tried calling my grandmother to tell her what happened, I actually lost the power of speech. My mouth moved in all the right ways, but no words came out. Tears streamed. Then I didn't cry a drop for three decades. I built an emotional shield around myself, strong enough to protect against a nuclear blast. I refused to be hurt again.

My parents had great love for my brother and me, but they both clearly struggled with their own demons. So I ended up trying hard to "check-out" and live more in my own head space than in the reality of life — which also meant I didn't want to be seen at all. It wasn't just that I was uncomfortable having people in my world; I didn't feel at ease in theirs, either. Birthday parties, slumber parties — they all freaked me out.

We're all products of our upbringing, good or bad, but the thing that differentiates us isn't where we come from but the path we carve ahead for ourselves. I wasn't comfortable in my own skin. But how could I like myself if I didn't even know myself?

Senior year of high school was my turning point. I got a job as a lifeguard at the Jersey Shore, and that gig became a real-life Baywatch moment for me. At the start of the summer, I was a gangly 6'4/185 pounds, but daily beach runs and ocean swims, along with some summer bronze, transformed me physically. I also achieved the most coveted physical asset that side of the Hudson River: a long, luscious mullet. It was the late 80s, and mullets were king. In retrospect, I realize this physical change attracted more of the attention I long sought — from the girls I wanted, from the friends I'd hoped to make — but at the time, I was oblivious. I still barely made eye contact and couldn't break free from my own distorted self-perception, but at least I started to relax a little. Ironically, some people even saw me as arrogant; but how can you be arrogant about something you can't see?

This transformation culminated with being elected student body president of my high school. It was validating — not because I suddenly thought highly of myself (remember: oblivious) but because I saw my win as a victory for all of us. Despite what my new lifeguard-toned body + super-mullet projected, I had always just been a dude most comfortable being lost in the crowd. Becoming school president gave a face to the people who weren't the quarterback or the all-star, the kids who never got their moment in the spotlight. I was them, with my acid washed jeans, shaggy mullet, and endless self-doubt. Me getting there meant *we* got there. My "everyone and no one" status made me the de facto bridge builder amongst these cliques, and my lack of identity worked in my favor in helping me to lead in that moment. But the pitfalls of operating without a compass caught up to me by college.

I credit New Jersey's proximity to New York as the catalyst for its prolific output of successful people, but perhaps not for the reason you'd expect. Yes, theoretically, access to big city resources through the Holland Tunnel favors ambitious Jerseyites, but I attribute the outsized impact of my Garden State brethren to one major factor: balls. Maybe it's something in the water? Whatever the cause, people from Jersey often have a willingness to risk, roll the dice, and lay it all on the line when they want something badly enough.

They say we never truly escape our teenage mental state. My Jersey upbringing and accompanying attitude has never left me. (Or let me escape from it.) It's an integral part of who I am. I own the fact that putting it nicely, I'm an acquired taste. Take me or leave me.

New Jersey in the late 80s was about as similar to Arizona State as Los Angeles is to Eastern Mongolia. I could not have chosen a more foreign place. Rocking my big gold rope necklace and "Sex Instructor: First Lesson Free" t-shirt, my image sharply contrasted the new world I stepped into, and nothing about me was a natural fit. Being "myself" never felt so wrong.

Arizona State was a giant, wealthy campus, where my freshman dorm was bigger than my entire high school. Some of the guys already owned Harleys — my dream in life! — at age 18. Everyone was gorgeous, and even the average ones were better looking than me. The girls — all blonde, by birth or by bottle — all seemed to know each other and hook up with the same cookie-cutter guys. Money oozed from people, including rich kids from California who partied too much to get into USC, so they settled for Arizona State.

Meanwhile, I was back to my high school pre-senior year insecurity. I'd cut my mullet just prior to college (thankfully), but its absence did nothing to help me assimilate. My horrific acne came to college with me. And glaringly missing from the college welcome packet was the insider tip to ditch the neon colors and acid-washed denim, which, apparently, had been deemed inferior to looking like a walking Ralph Lauren ad. I was a lost and wandering dipshit, studying the trust-fund-fueled homecoming kings like they were the masters of the universe. So I joined a frat, grew my hair into a preppy swoop, and even took a job at Banana Republic, just for the clothing discounts. The frat called me "brother", and my association with them earned me an invite to the big parties, and yet, nothing about these guys or events seemed comfortable or natural. I had neither the cash nor the cachet to fit in.

And that was my error: I was still young and moronic enough to think life was a competition against other people rather than myself. I was an insecure kid incapable of communicating the hurricane of inner thoughts and feelings that made my internal life as chaotic as my external existence. The existential crisis and insecurities that plagued me from a young age bubbled up from within, compounded further with each keg stand and Jäger shot, culminating with my nearly-dead Grateful Dead experience. A university education is supposed to be enlightening, but I came much closer to a 4.0 BAC than a 4.0 GPA in the six years it took me to complete my basic four-year bachelor's degree.

I explored transferring along the way but felt like a failure for even considering it. Every son longs to make his father proud, and I knew attending Arizona State made my father — a man who wasn't able to afford college for himself but still managed to become CEO of a publicly traded company he founded — extremely happy. It wasn't enough to just stay; I needed to *love* it. For him. But how?

I'd become isolated from my friends back home thanks in large part to the absence of today's technology and the ineptitude of snail mail. There was no internet to turn to, and therapy wasn't really a thing guys my age did (unless it was required by a judge after you fucked up really badly). So I was on my own. The only thing I disliked more than my daily existence at Arizona State was the thought of reporting back to everyone in New Jersey over the holidays. It was supposed to be incredible! How could I explain that I attended the Disneyland of colleges, and I wanted to get off the ride?

I needed to carve out a spark of creativity and disruption in my life that would set me free from the mindless, repetitive merry-go-round I was stuck on. I was craving proof that there really was something bigger and far more significant than my current reality.

Growing up, the sadness of others always resonated with me. Where there is great pain and sadness, I always believe there is great opportunity to help, and helping always fills me up. But what would be *my* positive contribution — beyond getting drunk and trying my hardest to get laid every fucking night? What meaningful role could I play? While I didn't have the answers, a fire was growing within me to embrace some type of genuine, meaningful pursuit that would make me a better human being and also positively impact the greater good. I wanted...I *NEEDED* to engrave this "self-pledge" somewhere as a constant, inescapable reminder. A promise to make good on that commitment — or be branded a liar. Forever!

I wanted a tattoo. (Hey, it was still a much bigger commitment than scribbling a note on a bar napkin.)

At the time, tattoos were not really on my radar. I'd seen photos, and some of the motorcycle guys had them, but none of my peers. Getting a tattoo would mean going rogue, which both unnerved and excited me. But I made a commitment, damn it! Placement was key: I decided on something high up on my leg, so you'd never see it unless I was naked or wearing really short shorts. It was my way of testing the waters of my own commitment, just flirting with stepping out of bounds, without openly diving head-first across that line.

After months of contemplation — but zero actual research — I stocked up on liquid courage and stumbled into a tattoo parlor a few blocks from my place. Of all the brilliant creative ideas and design inspirations in the world, I had none. ZIP. So I'd decided on a crying globe eyeball, which I convinced myself was a symbol of the suffering of others and a reminder to put my own struggles in context, hopefully sparking empathy over self-pity. Far beyond any emotional attachment to that design, it was the rush of permanence that struck me most profoundly. There was no (effective) tattoo removal back then, so I knew this thing was with me for life. There was no going back. I got off on the commitment — it was an actual high — making a decision beyond which keg party to hit up. The decisive-ness felt good. As did the fact that it was all mine — my idea, my secret. I didn't even think about the (extremely unfortunate) design until months, even years, after it was done. Some people jump off cliffs for a rush. The thrill of making a "forever" choice appealed far more to me — and still does. (Plus, I've always been scared shitless of heights.)

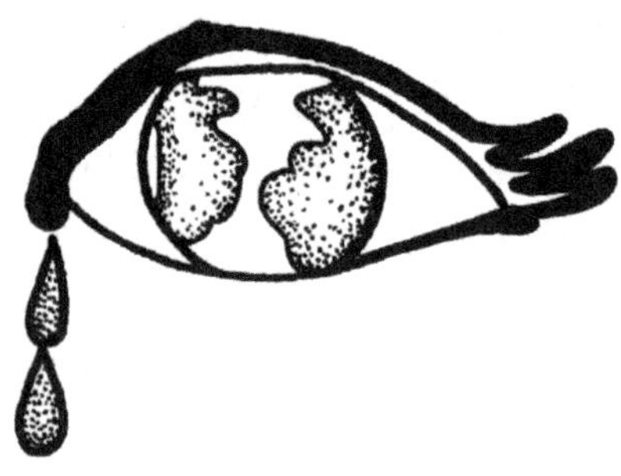

At the time, I didn't see this as the first of many tattoos. It wasn't about the tattoo at all. It was me busting out as an individual and breaking the mold of "normal," conforming, or status quo. It was a physical reminder of who I am and could still become beneath the skin in which I'd never felt truly at ease.

And yet, to this day, I cringe at this tattoo in much the same way I cringe at my awkward self back then. I omit it in conversation, never referring to it as my first tattoo. The design is closer to a first-grader's bad coloring job than to an artistic treasure. In fact, I didn't even want to talk about it in this very book (but my editor threatened to "out me" to the world if I didn't come clean). Couldn't we just skip ahead to the better ones?

But she was right. Anything less than 100 percent candid defeats the purpose — of my tattoos and this book. I've never considered myself a tattoo person. For me, each one is more of a practical, hard-earned rite of passage than an outlet for creative expression. No going back and re-writing history.

As odd as it may sound, I partially credit tattoos with restoring my faith and trust in people. Maybe your home life let you down, or your relationship failed, or your business went bust. A tattoo demands that you give yourself over to a stranger and give them the license to change something on your body *forever*. If that isn't trust, what is? I had very little faith in human beings as a kid, and with each "successful" tattoo, my belief in people grew. Tattoos have helped me believe in others *and* myself.

My tattoos are my bible. They're my testament to myself and the standards I set for myself. They're the living witnesses to whether I'm worthy of giving breath to the body they adorn. Tattoos don't make me or anyone a saint, but hopefully, they make me the slightest bit better than I would be without them. Or, at the very least, more aware. Some days, I come up (VERY) short. But even amidst my failures, my tattoos never leave, always reflecting back at me, pointing me forward. Always forward.

So don't shed a tear for my shitty thigh tattoo. We only get one virgin ink experience, and as much as I hate that crying globe, I would never remove it. We can upgrade from our past, but we don't need to hide from it.

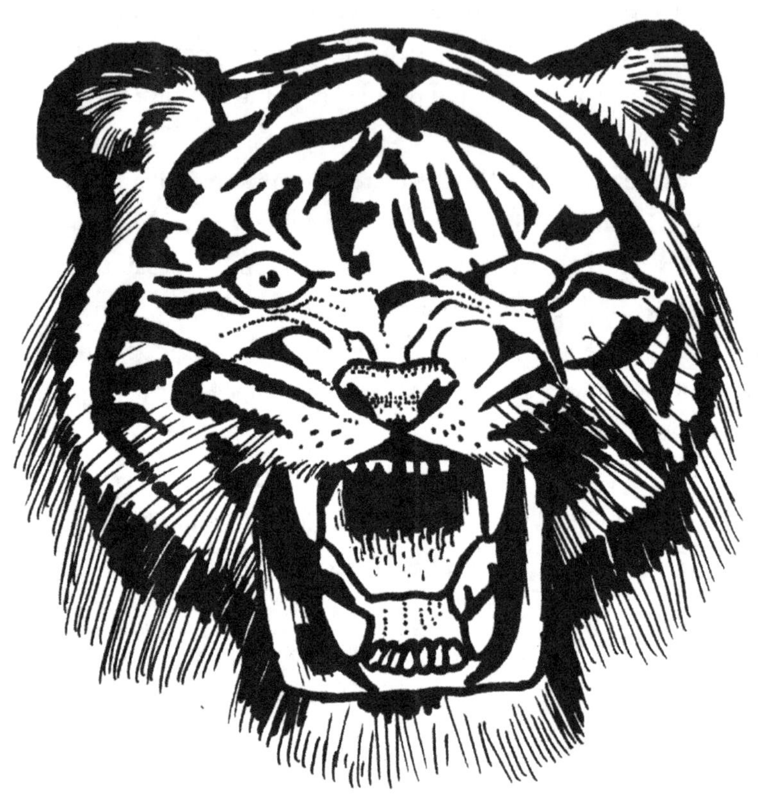

THE SCARRED TIGER by Jeff Johnson, Pastor, musician, YouTube vlogger

I went back and forth with my wife on what to get and finally settled on a tiger on my leg – my first leg tattoo. I wanted something fierce. I felt like it would be cool to put a scar on the tiger's face because I've gone through a lot of stuff in my life, and I've brought a lot of that stuff on myself.

There are scars that people see visually and scars that are metaphorical. Even though I'm scarred up, I'm still fierce. I'm still gonna do my thing. This tattoo is a reminder of my imperfections. I am not a good person. I have messed up a ton. And God still has a place for me.

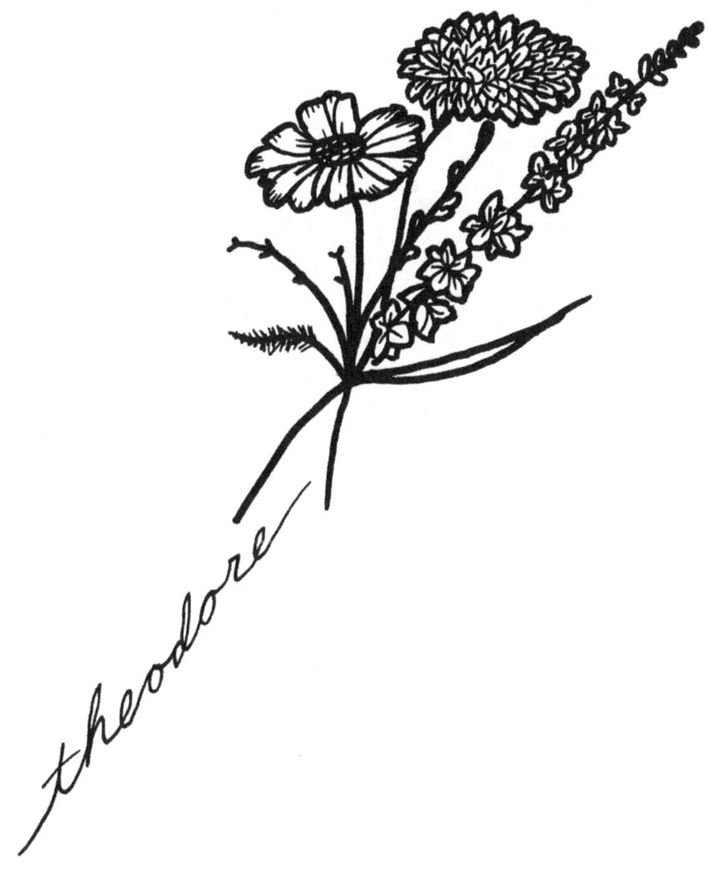

THE RAINBOW BABY BOUQUET by NATALIA JOHNSON, YouTube vlogger

Last year we went through a pregnancy that we were going to share with the world on our YouTube channel. Unfortunately, we lost that baby due to miscarriage. We already had two healthy babies, so this changed our perspective. There was no way to prepare for it emotionally. It's one of those things that there are no straight answers for. It takes time to heal.

After that miscarriage, we got pregnant with our "rainbow baby."

To mark this, I wanted a tattoo of a small bouquet of flowers. Daisies are the April birth flower, and that's when our son Theo was born. The baby we miscarried was due in July, which is a chrysanthemum, which means joy. I was going through a hard time in my life when I was pregnant with Theo, and he brought me so much joy once he was born. My kids are my joy.

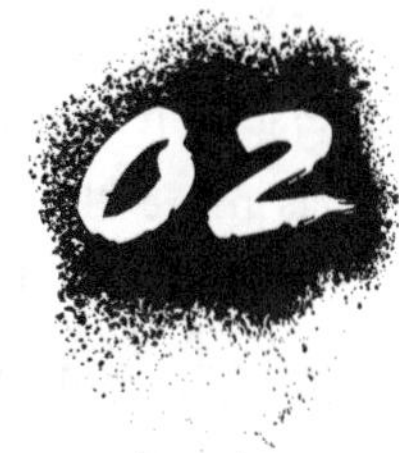

LEARN FROM THE PAST. LIVE FOR TODAY. HOPE FOR TOMORROW.

—ALBERT EINSTEIN

MAKING SHITTY VS. SHITTIER DECISIONS

Shocking reveal: the crying eye globe tattoo somehow did not cure me of all my problems or make me instantly enlightened.

After somehow managing to graduate from Arizona State's Walter Cronkite School of Journalism, I had it in my head that I wanted to be a TV news reporter. So after a couple of post-graduate years of full-time fucking around (even says so on my LinkedIn), I headed to Reno, Nevada to interview for what I thought was my dream job, writing and producing TV news, with the hope of working my way into a coveted on-air spot. This was my goal since high school.

Growing up, I was an atypical shy dude. In my mind, I thought I just sort-of slipped past people and blended in. In reality, I was hard to miss — visually and personality-wise. But my quest to be on TV wasn't about exposure or fame. It was more about the role TV played in society at the time: It was the primary medium for telling stories to a sizable audience. We got cable TV when I was in my early teens, which is where I discovered this new thing called CNN. Decades before networks became pawns for pundits and endless political rhetoric, CNN was the first 24/7 worldwide news machine with coverage from around the globe. Reporters doing live shots from war zones and sites of political upheaval, broadcasting mind-blowing images that became imprinted in our brains. As a teenager, I became fixated on the life of those reporters: They were adventuring, experiencing the stories that unfolded in front of them. The idea of being a journalist, especially a foreign correspondent, was not only exciting, but a mental escape to an entirely new world and place; a constant refresh of people, places, and cultures. That was the life I wanted, and becoming a TV reporter seemed like the best path to achieving it. Most people starting out in TV news want to be an anchor, helming The Today Show or GMA or the evening news. I had zero desire to become a desk jockey reading a teleprompter. That was fluff, fake entertainment to me. I wanted to go off the grid and interview inaccessible people and bring their remarkable stories to life, to tell the stories that nobody else would or could. There was no internet at the time, so other than becoming a newspaper reporter (and let's face it, grammar and spelling ain't my strength), TV was my ticket to achieving this dream.

In high school, I read an article that fascinated me. It was the story of Paula Cooper, a juvenile on death row in Indiana for committing a horrific murder when she was sixteen years old. I desperately wanted to interview her and tell her story or the story of someone in a similar position. Why, you might ask, did a sixteen-year-old middle-class kid from New Jersey want to speak to someone my age on death row? I guess, in part, it appealed to my sense of social justice. It seemed messed up to me that the United States was in the curious company of…Iran and Syria when it came to executing people for crimes committed as minors. Plus, the majority of these American juveniles on death row were often dealt a pretty shitty hand in their young lives — extreme poverty and hunger, severe physical and sexual abuse, unimaginable neglect. Did they deserve a medal for their brutal, criminal choices? Hell no! But at age 16, had I not already been guilty of making some pretty dumb fucking choices of my own without any real consequence? Uh…fuck yes (x100). Plus, it didn't take a rocket scientist to do some basic research and realize how biased the criminal justice system was against juveniles on death row like Paula. Not to mention the human brain is still developing as a teenager, including the ability to govern emotions and fully understand the consequences of actions.

After reading about Paula's case, I was struck by the senselessness of it all — not only her own unspeakable actions that took an innocent victim's life, but at the same time, the tragedy of her own life. What if my circumstances had been different? A little less fortunate, a little more fucked up? What horrific things might that have led me to do? Or many of us, for that matter?

I wrote dozens of letters to prisons (handwritten, sent via snail mail) requesting an interview with some of their juvenile death row inmates. Not surprisingly, most of them said "no" or didn't respond at all. But eventually, one dude on death row in Florida State Prison who committed first degree murder at the age of 17, inexplicably said yes, and I soon found myself on death row, sitting across from someone who could have been my classmate except for that fact that he was… awaiting execution. We sat a few feet from each other, him in handcuffs, no protective glass or barrier between us, with the camera rolling. We talked about the things kids our age talk about. He missed being around girls. His friends, sports… Were we really so different? Eventually, I asked him about his case and the murder that landed him on death row. The experience was surreal. I followed up that interview by tapping into my high school's public access TV channel, and like a mini Phil Donahue with a mullet, I created an entire talk show out of it, bringing in families of victims as well as actual cold-blooded convicted killers who had since been paroled, all discussing the issue of capital punishment on both sides.

(Side note: These days, as a large, fifty-year-old dude covered in tattoos and a full beard, when I tell people about my visit to death row, they typically step back and exclaim, "OMG! What did you do!? And how did you get released?" Then I get out the key words: "…as a sixteen-year-old journalist!")

So given this decade-long rehearsal and mental fixation on becoming a bona fide journalist, you can imagine how nervous I was for this Reno gig. It was 1998, and computers were not yet standard or mandatory. I couldn't type proficiently or use a computer with any functional skill, so I hand wrote some news copy for my in-person job interview and said none of the three computers worked. "They all work — you just don't know how to use them, do you?" Susan[1], the news director who interviewed me in Reno, rightly called me out. "But you do write good copy."

Reporters in Reno lived and breathed the news, and producers like me lived vicariously through the reporters' eyes. One day they would race up to Lake Tahoe for a press conference on the environment with the Vice President of the United States and the next they'd cover blazing fires in the field or report live from the grand opening of a massive new casino. It was a small town, but there's a reason Reno is known as the "Biggest Little City in the World." It felt like it, and I had a front row seat.

But being tied to a producer desk, I felt like the back-up quarterback. I hated it and counted the minutes until it was *my turn* to roll and operate in the action, on the *frontlines*, not the sidelines.

Within a year, the show I helped write and produce had been nominated for an Emmy. Having proven myself behind the camera, it was finally time for what had motivated me all along: my audition for an on-air spot. I knew the industry inside and out at that point. I was the voice inside the reporters' earpieces, and I understood what made great television. All I had to do now was stand up there and execute. The position was mine to lose, and my track record in those situations…was not great. In fact, *any time* something has been *mine to lose*, I've lost it in such a big fucking way, it's comical.

Exhibit A: Years ago, a new commercial project opportunity came along that was 1,000% in our sweet spot. My agency was MAAADE for this brand and campaign. It's like God showed up at my door and said, "Drew, I have created a campaign so perfectly suited to everything your agency excels at, THIS IS IT. You can't possibly fuck THIS up." The good Lord also attached the project to a huge, worldwide, publicly traded conglomerate with dozens of other mega brands in their portfolio. So I was fired up to be over-the-top prepared. My team and I ate, slept, and drank this brand for three weeks straight, building a presentation and

---

1   Name changed.

creative pitch deck that was seriously really fucking amazeballs. The president of the brand agreed and was so blown away with it, he decided not to pursue any other agencies. He KNEW we were his team for this.

There was one tiny last 'detail': Because it was a public company with a board of directors, and this was a huge financial commitment, he asked that we fly down to their corporate HQ in Florida to meet the board, show them the presentation, shake a few hands, "And then it's yours. Really, Drew, I never say this, but you guys have so impressed me, this is truly yours to lose." And he laughed.

I flew everyone in from L.A. an extra day in advance — I wanted to run through the prezo again (and again) on location. I joked with the team, "Lets acclimate to the temperature and air in Florida, so we feel calm and relaxed and at home when we meet the board and present." The night before the big meeting, I even did a dry walk through. LITERALLY. Meaning we walked from our hotel to the client's office, just to determine the exact time and distance. We were taking no chances. (We were stealth, walking over at night to ensure they wouldn't see our rehearsal walkover. 'Cause that would be embarrassing, right?)

The next morning, we were PREPARED. We walked into the front door, saw the signage (yup, we were in the right spot) and said hello to the receptionist — who, oddly enough, appeared to be the only human present in an otherwise large and empty office. She also had no idea why I was there. I stayed calm. I had this. I had looked up the address myself weeks earlier, so I whipped it out of my pocket and showed the receptionist. "OH, yes, I know who you are!" (I smiled. I knew it.) "Ummm, you're at the wrong location. Our main HQ is on the other side of…Florida. The board is expecting you there — right now." I guess instead of just Googling the corporate address, I should've looked more closely at the text the president sent me with the *actual* meeting address.

They needed about ten seconds to decide if the idiot who owned the agency (me) couldn't find their actual office for a meeting with their board, could he be trusted to lead their new multimillion-dollar campaign. Mine to lose. And I did.

So when the day came to test for the Reno TV reporter gig, it was pretty logical for me to think, "Don't fuck this up, don't fuck this up, *don't fuck this up.* You've been waiting for this your entire life." When they told me to start reading the fake news story for the fake camera, I'm surprised my first words weren't, "Hi, I'm Drew Plotkin reporting from Reno. DON'T FUCK THIS UP."

I sucked. Frozen, nervous, voice cracking and weak, devoid of any confidence. I put so much pressure on myself, obsessing so much over the possibility of failure, that I wasn't natural or authentic. I didn't connect with the camera or do any of the things I knew to do. I just froze, because I thought my entire life — my happiness, my success, every worthwhile aspect of it — hinged on this one moment. Who can possibly perform under that pressure? Not me. Not anyone. Nobody ever hit the winning home run in the World Series by walking up to the plate with their legs shaking, about to shart themselves.

Susan, the news director, never mentioned it again. But just moments after my flaming tailspin, she asked the dude sitting next to me if he wanted to audition for the same position — while I was sitting right there. He was thrilled, and I was fucking crushed. My head was spinning as I felt the world I'd hyped up in my mind collapse under me. It was her passive aggressive way of letting me know I fucked up that I would never forget. There was no recap of what happened. No conversation or discussion of where to go from here. Susan had been my boss and the person who believed in me enough to hire me, and yet, when I flopped face first in that audition, she dropped me. Ghosted me. Despite all the wins that year, that singular fuck-up was enough to convince her I was not worth any further meaningful investment.

We'd been nominated for an Emmy. I was legitimately good at my job. Did that mean I could be good at any job? No. But while I lacked experience, I was packed with passion. But there was no offer to mentor or coach me, to analyze what went wrong and how I could improve. Instead, she dismissed my aspirations. And…me.

That dismissal was one of the most motivating moments of my life.

Having *"Learn from the past. Live for today. Hope for tomorrow."* tattooed in Sanskrit on your arm is something you do in your 20s, not your 50s. You almost certainly have fewer tomorrows than yesterdays by the time you're 50. But one thing that remains the same is my aversion to being overly obvious. (As odd as that sounds coming from a heavily tattooed big dude who rides around in a Jeep with no roof or doors, chomping a cigar, with Springsteen blasting.) Just because I wear my life story on my flesh, doesn't mean I have to be an open book. I prefer to let my tattoos speak in code. On my arm is a tattoo of a Pericles quote in Greek: *"What you leave behind is not what is engraved in stone monuments, but what is woven into the lives of others."* On my shoulder, I tattooed a Mexican proverb (which originated from a Greek poet) in Spanish: *"They tried to bury us, they didn't know we were seeds."* The name of my oldest daughter's birth mother, written in her native Amharic (Ethiopian), and *risicare*, the Italian word "to dare" or "to chance," are inscribed on my arms. Do I speak or read these languages? No. But neither do most other people I encounter.

And then there's the Sanskrit of Albert Einstein's words: *"Learn from the past. Live for today. Hope for tomorrow."* As simplistic as it might seem, it has deep meaning for me, reminding me of my own life's pilgrimage. Learning from the past demands that we let go of the might-have-beens and focus on what is *now*. Where do we go from there? That's up to us. And some positive fucking vibes and hope never hurts.

I learned from an early age that life is often not as simple as yes/no, right/wrong. Often, it comes down to making a shitty versus an even shittier decision. Most people, when faced with a hard decision, make no decision at all. But avoiding decisions is a choice in itself. Most of us want to rise and even exceed the expectations (or lack thereof) of those around us. It's hard to break out of the mold of who people like to tell us we are, and what we are and aren't capable of. Every choice I've made in my adult life has been my own, good or bad. Yes, I shit myself in my on-air audition. No, I don't think I got a fair shake. But if success were predicated on fairness, we'd all be fucked.

While my official TV news career ended in an unceremonious flop, years later, I did finally achieve my (unofficial) role as journalist and storyteller — albeit not for any major news outlet. First, in a batshit-crazy-expedition to a remote Ethiopian village to try to help stop the murder of "cursed" babies (more on that later), and then again, far more accidentally, when I was featured on the Britney Spears documentary that helped break up the conservatorship case (I'll get to that later, too). Luck — or skill, depending how you look at it — weren't on my side in Reno. So it was up to me to change that.

My tattoos, in their obvious-yet-covert way, remind me daily to do something — *anything* — with the advantages I've been blessed with, and with the opportunities I can create. I may not be the greatest or the richest or achieve everything my adolescent heart desired. But I don't get to sit and sob about not making some childhood dream come true in whatever way I originally conceived it. Dreams change. Some die. Some are delayed. Some turn out even better than imagined. And some twist themselves like invisible contortionists into entirely new forms, leading us toward something completely off course from our previous life's radar. That's real hope, and, for me, real success: Getting off on the insanity of the unknown and not trying to stop it from crashing into you, regardless of the outcome.

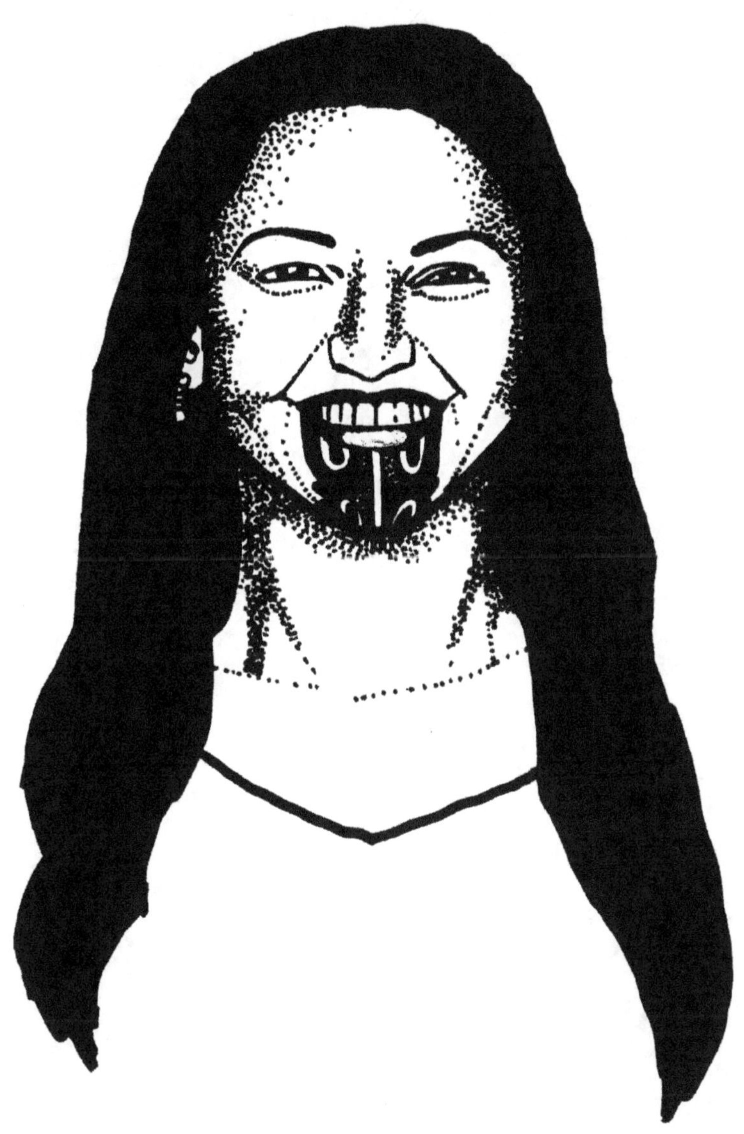

Ta moko is a sacred, traditional face tattoo among the Maori of New Zealand. In 2021, Oriini Kaipara became the first TV news anchor to appear on air with the tattoo.

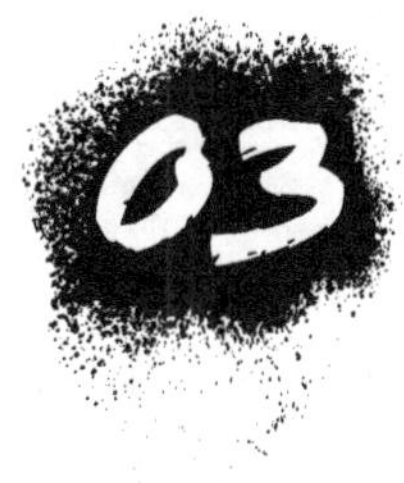

NO PLAN B
RESILIENCE TRAINING AND THE UNLIKELY WISDOM OF TELEMARKETING

*T*elemarketing can crush your soul. Or you can make it your bitch.

After my TV news career crashed and burned in Reno, I headed to California, where I found myself managing an apartment building in exchange for free rent. So while I had housing, I didn't have money. Meanwhile, my roommate was making $400-$500 a week selling financial investment newspaper subscriptions over the phone from a telemarketing office. He was a nice kid whose six-pack abs were his dominant skill-set, so I said to myself, *If he is making $500 a week doing this, I'll make $1,000. Easy.*

They hired me, and I started my mandatory two-week training period to learn the ropes. There was a lot they didn't teach me, however, so I staged my own personal training. I made a point of sitting next to the top sales guys on the floor, as well as the worst performers. People thought sitting next to the worst performers to train was dumb, but it made sense to me. Everyone tries to imitate the winners; I also wanted to learn from the losers to understand what to avoid. It wasn't just about understanding what people did right; I also needed to understand *where they went wrong.*

The sales room was a huge "open floor" office, with rows of guys and a few women stacked shoulder-to-shoulder at long desks with phones and headsets attached to them. Hearing the chatter of other salespeople around me was motivational, but what really fired me up was how they tracked performances in real time, making a public display out of the wins. A VERY big display. While still in training, I watched the sales manager call out the top performers, mentally committing myself to that number one spot.

My first week, I cracked the top three in sales revenue. When they announced the top performers and said my name, you could hear everyone murmur, *"Who?"* Nobody even knew my name — yet.

By the end of month one, I became the number one salesperson. Out of over one hundred reps, I held that position for eighteen months straight. My success surprised them so much that the managers started recording and listening to my calls because they assumed I must be lying to customers to close sales. When they confirmed there was nothing shady happening, they asked me to conduct live training sessions to allow the other reps to listen in.

The first time we did this, the new sales lead popped up on the monitor. It was in Alaska, which was considered a "+4 zone." That meant if they bought the paper, it would arrive in Alaska four days *after* it was printed. If you want a daily financial paper for playing the stock market — which is what we sold — receiving it four days AFTER the market closed was…less than ideal. The other hundred guys on the floor burst out laughing, because they assumed I was screwed and would fail. And damn, that really fired me up. To close it.

I sold the guy from Alaska a three-year subscription for about $400 (a sizable newspaper investment twenty-five years ago).

There were no circumstances too crazy for me to close. I once sold a woman a subscription who loved the paper, but previously canceled because the ink made her husband nauseous. (I kept her on the line long enough to tell her about our new online version — and helped her source a heavy duty, odor-tight garbage can to discard the physical papers upon arrival.) I sold a doctor a subscription by getting his nurse to read me his credit card over the phone while they performed a medical procedure. I averaged $4,000-6,000 per week for fewer than twenty hours of actual work.

How? I followed five simple rules that served me as well in telemarketing as they do in life.

- **Know when to go all-in and when to bolt**

As long as you believe you have a good product or service that the other person could genuinely benefit from, you have 90%+ of what you need to close the deal. But the key is knowing when to press on and when to avoid wasting your time and energy.

The first question I always asked on every sales call was, "How's your investing going these days?" There is so much in how this one question was phrased. It wasn't a yes/no option — it required an engaged response and one that was likely to provide more details and information. Information is the best tool to sell and close; without it, you are blind and wasting time — and *TIME* is your most precious commodity. (In business and in life.)

Maximizing your time follows one simple principle: Don't be a dumb-fuck. When somebody replied, "I'm not investing at all right now" or "I just got laid off. I wish I could invest, but I need to pay the mortgage," I would quickly thank them for their time and say, "I look forward to chatting when you get back on your feet — and back into the market." And then I was OUT. Why? Because someone who cannot use your product in a positive, useful manner — even if they wanted to — will either always say no (but they may burn forty minutes of your time shooting the shit with you first) OR they may end up saying *YES* (sort of). Some sales reps would see someone out of work as easy to manipulate. They could excite them with some BS *"This is your ticket back on your feet!"* pitch. "Mr. Jones, you can make so much money in stocks, you won't have to get a job again!" But that's a garbage deal and you're a garbage person if you do that to someone already struggling. Plus, they would likely cancel when they received the bill and you'd lose the commission — and be a total D-Bag in the process.

I believed then and still do today that it is always possible to win without making other people lose. Telemarketing — and life — are not zero-sum games.

- **Speak simply**

Other reps came from investment backgrounds, some were even former stock brokers. And as odd as it sounds, this often worked against them. When I observed the worst performing reps, I realized most were not dumb or uninformed. Quite the opposite: Most were TOO informed. Or at least too eager to make sure the person on the other end of the phone knew how "brilliant" they were. Some reps spent half an hour on the phone walking through the paper, page by page, pointing out all the details and nuances and *over*-educating them. They never STFU, or asked questions, or LISTENED. I had a simpler approach:

"Ms. Rogers, you said a moment ago you do invest, and you buy four to six different stocks per year, correct?"

"Yes, I'm a small, simple investor. I really only buy a handful of blue chip stocks, and I typically buy and hold because I travel often and don't want to be glued to my desk reading investment newspapers all day — so this paper really isn't for me."

"I agree, you have better things to do! Hey, before I let ya run, quick thing: we do now offer the paper online, as well, and you get the website access FREE with the paper when you travel. Do you think a paper like this, with online access, would help you make at least one stock decision this year that would gain you, say…at least two points in price? Or save you from a two-point drop?"

"Oh yes, of course. How could it not at least help that much?"

"Good, because two points up or down on one single stock this year more than covers the entire cost of the subscription."

"You know, that makes so much more sense when you put it that way…"

No BS. No over-complications. I assessed the opportunity and acted fast and smart, by keeping it simple — an approach that benefits most things.

- **Embrace rejection**

Yes, there was some sales skill and product knowledge involved, but at the end of the day, like many (many) things in life, it was also a numbers game. And making the numbers work in your favor takes mental toughness. In any arena.

Imagine you're sitting in a soul-sucking, bland office, absent any life or personality — or hope, for that matter — with one hundred other fairly miserable people. Your days consist of endless calls, and the vast majority of those calls lead to rejection. I don't care how charming or smooth you think you are, you're getting rejected a huge percentage of the time. It sucks, but it's a statistical fact. Some people will be rude and yell or hang up on you. The occasional person will politely decline — but don't get too used to that. No one dreams of becoming a telemarketer when they grow up, just like no one wants to talk to one on the phone.

Back in the 90s, most telemarketing was heavily commission-based, which meant it was normal for people to spends hours on the phone being rejected and not get paid for it: no sales, no money. But that was the failure mindset, the "why always *meeeee*" whiner mentality. Feeling sorry for yourself is the kiss of death in any situation. And let's be real: You *know* if you fall into this category or not. You can lie to anyone and everyone, including your dog, but you can't lie to yourself on this one. The truth is MOST of us fall into this category at some stage in our life, including me. The key is breaking out of that slump. And the good news is that's something we *can* control. It's a simple personal choice, followed by a simple mindset adjustment.

Ninety percent of my fellow sales reps were recovering addicts — booze, drugs, both — and most of the sales team came from referrals from people who attended AA meetings. So the sales floor was occupied by a lot of unique characters from some colorful walks of life. There was a chiropractor whose pill-popping habit cost him that career, former real estate brokers, stock traders, entertainers, school teachers, former military and law enforcement, a pilot — nearly all were recovering addicts. I remember one guy who was doing well, earning over $1,000-2,000 in weekly commissions but had to drive to Verizon to prepay for cell phone usage because his pre-sobriety heroin habit shredded his credit.

So these dudes were no strangers to genuinely overcoming serious adversity and circumstances that might otherwise feel "unwinnable." And yet, many of them took it personally anytime they didn't sell…a newspaper. It was a type of personal rejection for them — the same as it would be for most people in the world. But the ten percent of us that had zero fear of rejection? We made the real money. And week after week, it was always the same group. Why? Because when others whined and bitched and whimpered, we laughed, joked, and got more fired up to close the next one. Just like in life. (To be clear, some of the most successful sales reps were, in fact, recovering addicts. My point being: rejection can wreak havoc on anyone if you don't apply the right mindset, even if you are someone who has previously demonstrated the ability to overcome significant obstacles under different circumstances.)

Example: When a lead said, "I'm not interested, but thank you," I would hear other reps whine and even beg: *"Please, Mr. Smith, I earn a small commission if you buy the paper, and it would really help me out."* That pity purchase might work on one person, but not consistently. I, on the other hand, would hear "not interested" and say, "No problem at all. Hey, before I let ya run, mind if I ask: what are the top one or two things keeping you from buying the paper today?" Then I would STFU and *LISTEN* — and they would tell me. I could almost always overcome any valid issue or concern they had, but *only if I actually took the time to hear what the objection was.*

If you don't know what isn't working, you can't fix it. If you want to be a mind-reader, join the carnival and put up a booth. Mind reading is not for me. I deal in reality and action with a purpose. And that requires *asking questions* and *listening.*

- **Find motivation through gamification**

The sales floor was a rush for me, and while it wasn't my TV news dream job, I somehow found a way to enjoy it. That started with never seeing it as "telemarketing." Instead, I saw it as a *sport*: It was high intensity thrill seeking, and every sale I closed was a fucking RUSH. Sounds lame compared to skydiving or racing cars or whatever people do for an adrenaline high. But for me, I loooooved closing sales. It was a path to winning…proving myself to me… over and over again, every day.

Most of my peers believed if they didn't make a sale for two or three hours, that meant they worked for free and had wasted their time. WRONG. Sure, I had dry streaks — we all do. But what gave me an edge was seeing every person who rejected me as a helpful step closer to those who would NOT reject me. *When you reject me, you get me that much closer to an inevitable win.* In some of the group trainings I've done for sales teams, I've started the session by having the group chant repeatedly with me, "We LOVE rejection!" Besides being a fun icebreaker to kick off a training, there's a simple and hugely valuable lesson in embracing rejection.

- **Go all-in**

Most people hide from potential rejection in all aspects of life. Why? Because rejection usually hurts. Some more than others. A successful person gets to the heart of a rejection or any sort of objection as fast as possible. Because we know it's there, somewhere. Pussyfooting around objections only burns more of your precious time and hampers your potential achievement. Plus, once I find out what your objection is, I can often overcome it — IF I have the passion and skill-set to address it.

Does this work one hundred percent of the time? No. Does it work a shit ton (actual metric measuring term) more than people could ever imagine? Well…I worked at this same telemarketing gig for eighteen months. I had never been a telemarketer in my life and didn't know jack or shit about investing or financial education, which is what we were selling with the newspaper. And yet, I was the number one salesperson every single month I was there. Everyone thought I had a magic saying, or a trick, or some kind of secret. The only thing I had was a very committed mindset, a simple action plan (that was heavy on listening and human connection), and a passion for success.

Some people struggle to see what a strong mental outlook and action plan looks like. Everyone has their own set of unique skills. Some, yes, have more than others. Some are blessed with superior abilities and attributes. In most ways, I was not one of those people. I fall under the category of having very few "natural" skills. But I perceive that as a positive, because knowing this about myself, instead of feeling sorry for 'poor me', I simply go deeeep. Always. On everything. For most of my life, in most aspects of life. I'm one thousand percent in or I'm out. Nothing halfway. (So I probably should have predicted that first tattoo would lead to covering my entire body…)

As kids growing up in New Jersey, we got into fights. It was normal. I'm not talking about weapons or bullying. It was kids being kids, throwing some punches, then reverting back to being friends again the next day. I was not a great technical brawler, but I had heart. When I got knocked down (which was often), I got up faster than anyone else, and said, "You will have to kill me to keep me down." I meant it. I've never had an off-switch or a backwards option. I may go to the left or to the right to find another path to victory, but I will never go backwards or quit. Perseverance, resilience, commitment, dedication. These are my skills. They're also personal mental choices, not inherited attributes.

✦ ✦ ✦

no plan b

There was no "Plan B" on the sales floor. You either made the sale or you didn't. And while I was smart enough to know there would always be some deals I would lose, I was not willing to fail. It was not in my vocabulary or mindset. So instead of "doing the math" on two or three bad hours with no sales, I always waited to do my math until I knew I was OK with the balance, be it at the end of the day or the end of the week. I knew the big picture always looked great, if I just pushed through the obstacles.

I've always lived a "No Plan B" life, which is why I tattooed it on my left index finger. I never quit. But it's not as simple as "don't quit." More than anything, living your life with a "No Plan B" mindset is about the inner drive and relentless passion to WIN and SUCCEED. I don't want to just tear down obstacles in my path; I want to transform and rebuild them into bridges I can ride across all the way to victory.

Nobody enjoys rejection (unless rejection is some fetish I'm unaware of). But it is a reality in every facet of life — work, play, relationships…it's part of the human condition. Telemarketing taught me not to fear rejection, because rejection was a guarantee. When you start to accept that as a general reality, you can allow yourself to take it less personally. That allows you to actually listen and dissect objections. So you can overcome them.

Most of my fellow reps couldn't handle getting hung up on repeatedly, day in and day out. This can either beat you up and spit you out, OR it can teach you the value of rejection. I learned to get the "nos" out of the way so I could open up the space for the "yeses."

We need to get to the "no" faster in life. You can't remove the roadblocks you don't know exist.

Telemarketing taught me far more than my journalism gig did. And many are embarrassed to admit to having a job like that. But for me, it was the opposite of a dead-end job. It was my professional path to resilience training.

Everyone loves to talk about resilience — who has it, how you get it, how to raise kids with it. And yet, resilience is as misunderstood of a commodity as bitcoin.

In college, there was this guy who always pulled the super attractive girls. He's not what you're picturing. He was short — probably 5'7 on a good day. Soft dad bod (which was not a big selling point at ASU), underwhelming hair. No horns coming out of his head, but not particularly good looking. No stand-out sense of style or flashy status signifiers. And yet, he was always dating beautiful girls. Nothing added up. I was always trying to figure out his angle. Did he have a lot of money? A nice ride? The best pickup lines? One day, I finally asked him, "So… *how?*" He said, "You know what, I go up to one hundred girls a day and ask them out. Ninety-nine of them say no. Some just keep walking or tell me to fuck off. But one will say yes. That's it. All I need is one to say yes."

Right there, talking to this exceptionally average guy, I found a key piece of the inspirational mindset that helped shape my own perspective on resilience. He was generally considered unnoticeable, but that didn't shake his confidence. He wasn't slick, he didn't lie to women, but he approached so many girls that his nerves no longer feared rejection. He was just calm and relaxed — comfortable in his own skin. And persistent: *He got to the no, so he could find the yes.*

The yeses are always out there — if you look long and hard enough and have the right mental fortitude and perspective. I'm living proof.

My stint as a telemarketer cemented the "99 out of 100" rule and allowed me to apply it to almost everything. Early in life, if someone said "no" when I asked them out, I would immediately think there was something wrong with me — to the point where I didn't ask people out, because I was so concerned about the potential (likely) rejection. But over time, I not only became less concerned about failing, I welcomed it. I knew it was not a step back, but one step closer to where I wanted to be. It allowed me to walk away from what wasn't right for me, be it a girlfriend or potential client or business partner. This took years to learn and accept, but to this day, 99/100 dude remaines a constant voice in my head if any type of doubt ever sneaks in.

Some of the best things I've accomplished in life have had odds far more daunting than 100-to-1, including a career directing some of the biggest celebrities and pro athletes and a robust portfolio of brands at the agency I built, along with the non-profit I helped launch that brought countless wheelchairs to severely disabled children around the world. I'm so comfortable with ridiculous odds that "long shots" don't feel all that long to me. Chances are, I've already been a helluva lot further out there in no man's land and back again.

THE WORKING MAN

Elvie Shane,
Country singer of #1 hit "My Boy"

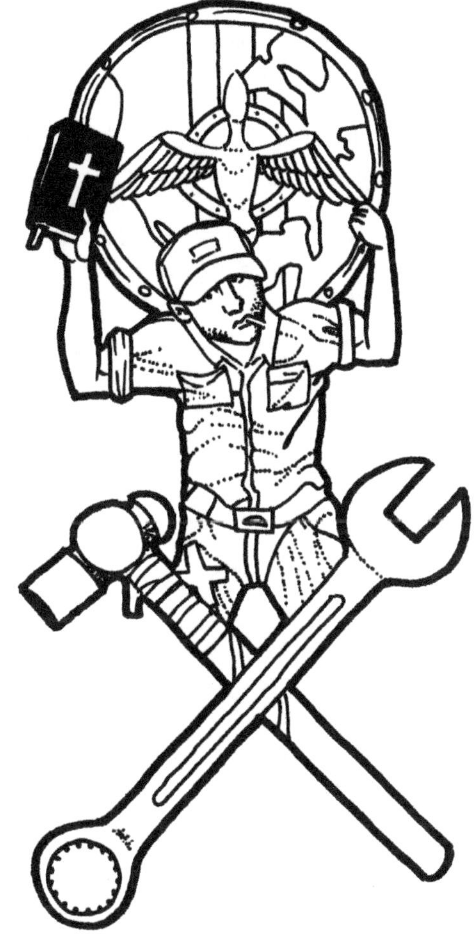

This tattoo is a tribute to my grandfather. We lost him to lung cancer right after Covid started. This dude was up every morning at 4am his entire life, put his boots on at four in the morning and didn't take them off until ten at night. He was a dairy farmer and a Marine Corps drill instructor for years. I never heard him say a cuss word in my life. He was the strongest guy I ever met.

He's the biggest example for me of "you don't know what you've got 'til it's gone." He lived so far away that I only saw him one week a year. Ever since he passed away, I realized little things that I learned from him. Most of it is about working hard and trying to be a good person.

This is also a tribute to the working man. Everyone I ever grew up around, and all the lessons I learned, were from the working man. With this tattoo, you've got a guy in a blue collar outfit, he's got the weight of the world on his shoulders – and I know how that feels sometimes. I'm just a blue collar working man myself, and I hope to be a voice for those people with my music.

There's a code in here, on the tattoo, that I put into this design for a card trick that my grandpa made up in the Marines. He taught it to me and all his kids and grandkids, but I'm only allowed to teach it to my kids and my grandkids. One day when I teach them, I'll be able to show them the code within the tattoo. Maybe this tattoo will be one that gets passed down. We'll see.

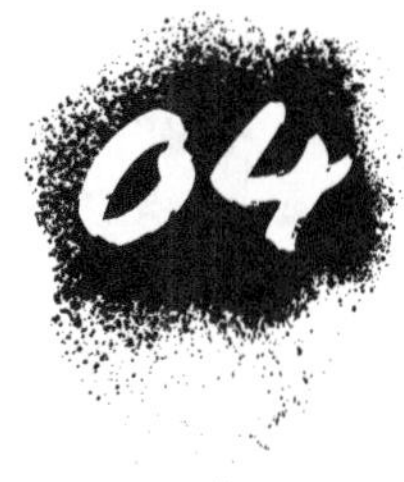

BUT WAIT, THERE'S MORE!

THE INFOMERCIAL OF MY LIFE

A few years ago, some people visited my agency. Our office was packed. We'd grown to about 35 employees, all jamming out, working on TV and digital campaigns for well-known brands. We viewed ourselves as more of a creative think tank than a formal agency. One of the visitors remarked, "Wow, Drew, this is so impressive. How did you get started? Film school? Did you have connections?" I laughed and shook my head: "No — I told a yoga guy I wanted to make an infomercial with him." That was not the response he expected.

In the late 90s and early 2000s, infomercials were still a new and rapidly growing sales format, thanks to media deregulations in the 1980s that paved the way for them. At the outset, it was mostly hocus-pocus psychic network gibberish. But by the 90s, a few people realized this infomercial thing was the golden fucking goose on crack. If you were balding, overweight, or wanted to look younger (FAST!), then infomercials were the yellow brick road for consumers, while producing bricks of gold for marketers.

It's impossible to compare infomercials to anything today, as there are now a stream of new platforms begging for your marketing dollars at any one time. By the time you master YouTube and Instagram, you move on to TikTok, then Pinterest becomes hot again, so you circle back to it… Plus, today, you're optimizing for multiple formats all at once — desktop, mobile, tablets, and countless different social platforms. But not back then. It was pretty much just TV, so you could really hone your craft and go deep. (And remember, going deep was my skill or natural gift).

The infomercial had a rather simple premise to success: It's 2am. You're awake. WTF ya gonna do? Fliiiip the channels. And I knew the power of the flip. That's why I've always been psychotic about the first few seconds of my half-hour infomercial campaigns. I knew I had three seconds max to get you to NOT HIT THAT FUCKING REMOTE BUTTON AGAIN. *STAY WITH ME, BABY!*

At the height of the infomercial craze, I had recently moved to California and was managing an apartment building, living rent free. It was not in the best area. Not safe for walking after dark, and you had to ignore the bullet marks on the garage. (I remember walking a date through the garage to my apartment when she asked about those marks. I convinced her it was the work of a famous sculptor I asked to do a "garage-art" favor for me.) At one point, one of my tenants was a week late on rent and not responding to "pay or quit" notices, so I used the manager's key to open the door. I found the dude dead on his chair with a crack pipe by his side. The nasty smell and appearance revealed he'd been dead for days. So yeah, it wasn't glam, but I was living rent free.

To make money to live (before discovering telemarketing), I bartended at night in West Hollywood. At the bar, I was surrounded by celebrities and power brokers in the entertainment industry, but couldn't figure out how to break in. I was still bruising — mentally and physically — from my failed stint in Reno. The stress of it all gave me chronic neck pain, so I went to see a doctor in Santa Monica. He was a general family doctor, and after looking at my chart, said, "You've been to Mayo Clinic, physiotherapy, half a dozen chiropractors, an assortment of specialists — why do you think I can help?" Fair point. As I was leaving, certain

I'd wasted my afternoon and a co-pay I couldn't afford, he said, "Ever do yoga?" "Uh, the thing where people wear sheets and turbans and chant 'Ommm?'" I asked. He laughed, "Well…sort of. But there is a yoga studio up the street from here that is a different kind of yoga — fast, powerful, sweaty, a great physical workout." I was slightly interested, but then he said the magic words: "Oh, and the classes are loaded with really pretty women. Models, actresses. And some really fit guys who want a killer workout." I was already out the door after "pretty girls." I ran straight to the yoga studio, only to find a line around the corner. Seal, Elisabeth Shue, David Duchovny, Jeremy Piven, some of the ER actresses. All in as promised, some very, VERY beautiful women. Good enough for me. Plus, I was desperate for neck pain relief.

I'd seen the place before. It was a little hole in the wall over a dingy Radio Shack on Santa Monica Blvd. It always had a line of gorgeous, fit people snaking out the door. I had always just assumed it was a photo studio doing a casting call. So I joined the line to see if this 'special yoga' was really worth the wait.

After one class, I was all in. I ended up taking two weeks of classes, after which my neck was essentially cured. The flowing workout, the energy, the instructor, the people it attracted — I'd never experienced anything like it. I knew instantly it was different, and I also knew anyone who got a taste of it would be as hooked as I was.

One night, around that time, I was watching TV on my shitty rabbit ears antenna and saw an infomercial for Billy Blanks' Tae Bo exercise program. I changed the channel, but it was also on half of my other six channels. And again the next night. And the next.

Then…BOOM.

I put the two together and what came next was so simple: I would make an infomercial with yoga dude to offer the world VHS video cassettes of his class.

So the next day, I went to the public library and photocopied a manager's talent agreement. I didn't own a computer and had no clue how to build or rep a brand — plus, there was still no "product" to sell. He was just a yoga teacher, and you can't sell that. But if I could be his *manager*, I figured I would be tied to whatever we came up with to market him to the world.

Fortunately, yoga dude was cool with that idea. He was making a FORTUNE teaching, but — cleverly — he didn't charge for the class. It was all "donation only"...which was brilliant. By saying "free yoga class: donate what you want," the vast majority of this karmic crowd of yogis would donate much more than if he actually charged a set fee. I remember watching him count the donation box on numerous occasions. It was insane. He had a killer house up in Topanga, cars, a motorcycle, traveled extensively, dated celebs — all on "free" yoga. (His accountant also managed money for high profile celebs. I'd have to guess financial advisors at that level don't usually work with destitute yoga teachers if they're only scraping by on nominal donations.)

After we signed our manager deal, it was not a fast-track to success. I spent two long years sending out press kits, calling any company in America I thought might, for whatever reason, be interested. I networked at any event that would let me in and talked about it with all my customers at the bar. I was obsessed with getting yoga guy an infomercial deal that would include the production of a VHS workout video. Tae Bo was my model, and I knew if people would buy that, there was likely an appetite for other new workouts. (Plus, I did some seriously comprehensive, market research, which, in its entirety, was as follows: If Tae Bo could afford to run so many freakin' times a day, on so many different freakin' channels, they had to be selling gazillions of fucking videos. I mean, who could argue with such thorough analysis?)

Eventually, I scored a solid meeting with one of the larger established infomercial companies at that time. The meeting was scheduled and rescheduled five times over several months, and when ya only have one actual prospect, those are some massive curveballs and emotional rollercoasters. I finally got confirmation of a firm locked-in date that actually seemed like it was really gonna happen. So, I did what any budding Hollywood manager would do: I went to Men's Wearhouse to buy a sports coat. I certainly didn't own one. As the sales guy rang up my purchase, he mentioned I could get a second sport coat for fifty percent off. I laughed and told him I just needed it for this one BIG meeting. "What if it goes well?" he asked. "There will be a follow-up meeting. You don't want to look like you only own one coat, right?" As a fellow salesperson, I had to respect his game. And he did have a point. So, of course I walked out with two new sport coats — for one meeting.

Fortunately, the big meeting DID happen. Boom! Chest bump. It felt amazing walking out of it. I was in the big leagues now. A player long before there were ballers. I couldn't wait to call my father and tell him how it went. I went to bed on top of the fuckin world — 'til the next day, when I got the standard Hollywood call: "We loved your presentation. It just isn't the right project for us right now. But good luck." I never did wear that second sports coat.

In better news, I was scheduled to move to a nicer apartment in Santa Monica. I guess I collected the rent and changed light bulbs well enough to earn a promotion to a much nicer place to manage — and still live for free. That meant I was only a few blocks away from the actual yoga studio…*aka, my entire client roster.* I could more easily squeeze in my number one client for an occasional lunch or "business meeting" to discuss our brand. Plus, I was making money bartending at night, and pretty soon, dove into my telemarketing gig. The big meeting might not have landed me a "yes," but things were still improving.

Then I got a call from one of the countless random press kits I'd mailed out. A REAL, legit company with REAL, legit infomercials on TV. They wanted to visit a yoga class and meet yoga dude and me in person. Shortly after that first visit, we landed our deal. It even included an advance of $10K! Which means, with my manager fee of ten percent, my nearly two years of work and several thousand in out-of-pocket expenses had earned me… $1,000! YES!!!!!

Sure, that sounds about as wonderful as a hernia check from a doctor with an over-tight grip, but I was officially making money in the infomercial world! I was living rent free, making good money bartending, and by this time, bringing in around $5k most weeks from the telemarketing gig, but that $1,000 was really a career jolt that felt like millions. I was RICH, 'cause I finally had a path. Something tangible I could wrap my head and passion around and focus on as a career. And the infomercial biz was a "sky's the limit" type of industry back then. Enough inventors and TV personalities were getting rich off it to prove to me there was untapped money to be made. And now I had my foot in the door.

Unfortunately, it turns out the one big thing a free manager's agreement from the library doesn't do for you is protect you. So it was not too hard for yoga guy's money manager to "work around me." It was a lifetime ago, and while I was pissed and ready to go to war back then, the reality is, the infomercial itself flopped anyway. It was released right around the same time the company financing our deal went bankrupt due to a downtown in the ecomony along with some other bad investments they made before our campaign ever even launched. We never stood much of a chance, as the execs were all running for the lifeboats and pointing fingers, just as we started to air-test on national television.

BUT…I *did* add one small provision to that shitty library contract in advance — and that clause changed my life: It guaranteed not just roundtrip airfare and accommodations for yoga dude on all infomercial shoots and locations, but also for his beloved *manager*, yours truly. So during the filming of the yoga infomercial, which happened all across the country, in an effort to show America how "mainstream" yoga was twenty-five years ago, I was embedded with the production team. And I soaked it up. Absorbed all of it. The technical aspects — cameras, lights, locations, logistics — to the creative process, the execution, script writing, directing, who does what on set, who is called what on set, where to get a snack, what to do and — just as important — what NOT to do. It turned out the producers filming our infomercial were an exceptionally gifted group that already produced other $100 million dollar campaigns. So in addition to my $1,000 for two years of work, I scored hands-on, real-time education in a very condensed period of time, which was priceless. To this day, I jokingly refer to that window of time as "when I got my MBA in infomerciology." (I tend to find many MBA types to be entitled, pompous, arrogant, do-nothing ass fungus — and those are the ones I like.) This was my no-BS, knuckles grinding, feet-to-the-fire MBA. It was the last certificate of higher learning I would ever seek.

Shortly after the yoga flop, I was introduced to a skincare company that had allocated a $1M budget — HUGE money 25 years ago — for an infomercial promoting their new acne line. They hired some big agency to film it, paid for all the agency fluff and BS money could buy. Mostly a bunch of wannabe "creatives" with a degree, who couldn't sell used underwear at a garage sale catering to perverts. So, big surprise, that VERY expensive infomercial failed miserably. They didn't even attempt to fix or edit it. They had to start from scratch.

When I met the brand execs, they were desperate for a fast, cheap fix. (*Fast and cheap.* If I had a real company name back then, that would have been it.) When I reviewed the Titanic of all infomercials, I observed something: It really sucked. It was even worse than the awful results suggested. The whole premise of this nearly thirty-minute-long diatribe was based on convincing the viewer how REAL and NOT FAKE the actual results were from their acne product. In fact, the previous team in charge was so obsessed with their "vision and creative genius," that they lost sight of the basics. They produced an entire million-dollar commercial that was not actually a commercial. It was a hybrid of "how to film results without cheating" and "look what we learned in film school," all rolled into a half hour snoozathon that would have put a coked-up narco to sleep in fifteen seconds.

So my "fix" was to do the total opposite. I went down to the Third Street Promenade in Santa Monica and filmed real people trying our acne product while our cameras rolled. Instead of hiring glam looking models — which was the norm in the industry — I drafted real customer service agents from the actual acne brand so they could speak to real acne sufferers with both intelligence and compassion. We took photos, interviewed the acne "testimonials" who would be testing our brand, handed them product, then brought them back in four weeks later to film them again. We didn't "educate the viewer" on lighting techniques or try to convince them the competitors were fakes or show measuring tapes and distance from the camera to the pimple (yes, they did). We let real fucking people with real acne talk and share their real stories. Uninterrupted. Unscripted.

And ya know what happened? Real people out shopping on a typical L.A. afternoon, who in a completely unplanned turn of events, became our testimonials, burst into tears when they talked to us. Acne is real. It's embarrassing. It hurts. It makes us insecure and self-conscious. It isn't about the director or film techniques or production values or sets. It's about human beings and their true feelings and emotions. And when these real people started to cry, we kept roll-ing — we didn't call for an assistant to "fix the makeup," and we didn't tell them what to say or what not to say. We let them be *THEM*. Plus, I shared something personal with them off-camera: That I suffered with horrendous acne throughout high school and on-and-off in college. I shared some of my personal stories of humiliation and embarrassment, including the time in college I chose to take an "F" on a public speaking project rather than deliver my presentation on a specific day when my face was a pepperoni pizza (with extra pepperoni). The experience was raw, honest, and vulnerable. And they knew and appreciated that. I wasn't a director in that moment. I was a dude with a history of embarrassing acne who could relate to their hurt and emotions. So they trusted me. And I never took for granted the trust I *earned* on every project I personally directed and oversaw. (*Earned*. Never demanded or felt it was OWED. I earned it.)

The footage we shot for a tiny fraction of that original budget was so compel-ling, the skincare company asked us to edit it into an infomercial. We turned their infomercial bomb into a mega-hit. For many years, our campaign raked in tens of millions in sales, won awards, and opened up my eyes to the way that skincare and personal care products could connect emotionally with people in a positive, non-shaming format.

Thanks to my agency's name rolling in the credits, I became in-demand and easy to find. I soon connected with Tony Horton of P90X fame. These were hard, extreme workouts and definitely not for everyone. So they enlisted me to make a more "inclusive" option. We called the new version the "10 Minute Trainer" ('cause if an ass-kicking one-hour P90X workout is too scary, then how about a nice, happy 10-minute training session with Tony?) 10 Minute Trainer instantly became the new number one infomercial in America. I didn't just have a path to a LEGIT career, but I had the number one show. Flip any channel and — boom! There was MY commercial. I would stop at bars and anywhere that had TVs on just to watch my own damn commercial I'd already seen 1,000 times. Gyms? Loved 'em, 'cause they've got 100 TVs hung from the ceiling, often on the same channel, so I could work out while my infomercial blasted on thirty different TV sets up above. (Aside from the confidence boost, getting monthly royalty checks also didn't suck. A lot fucking better than selling newspapers in a telemarketing office!)

Now, instead of mailing out one hundred press kits and cold calling companies for an introduction, companies were calling *ME*. I hadn't even figured out how to market or advertise myself when I realized I didn't need to. These nationally-broadcast infomercials *were* my advertisements. My shows were my business cards. I became known as an obsessive freak who traded traditional, outdated methods of shooting infomercials for my own unorthodox methodology that came with a freakishly high success rate.

For example, a global company had a vacuum infomercial showcasing a great product, but no one was purchasing it. Why? This unique vacuum did EVERYTHING. It practically drove your kids to school, it was so fucking advanced. And simple to use. The company had filmed three separate infomercials with various production agencies and marketing teams trying to crack the code. It was always close, but never a winner. So what was the problem? I became obsessed with figuring that out.

So I camped out inside various Best Buy stores and spent hours (and hours) watching people buy vacuum cleaners. They checked labels, read the tags, lifted them, touched them, rolled them around. Once someone made their pick, I asked them, "Why this one?" Obviously cost is always a variable, so I didn't get too caught up on that, but at the end of the day, the answer was what any second grader would guess right every time: SUCTION. "We want a vacuum cleaner that suctions up all the crap. And keeps sucking, without clogging every two minutes." "Well, sir, do you like this one that is lightweight?" "I do. But the one I'm buying has better suction." "Ma'am, did you notice this one also cleans up wet spills?" "Yes, I did, and I like that a lot. But this one has a stronger, longer lasting suction." "But did you see this one over here with 500 different attachments?" "Oh yes, and those would be wonderful, but my last vacuum had terrible suction, so this time I need to make sure I get one with the *best* suction."

The problem with the original infomercial was, yes, consumers liked all the bells and whistles, but it also convinced them that those bells and whistles *compromised* suction. And people buy vacuum cleaners 'cause they love things that suck.

Good, hard, and continuously. (Yeah, I'm still talking about infomercials.) It's truly that simple. So I re-edited the infomercial without even shooting a frame of new footage, but with suction as the clear and overwhelming primary power house benefit. Purchases jumped by 400 percent.

From then on, my biz dev was on autopilot. In my entire agency career, selling over $1 Billion over various products and services for countless brands, I never had a business card. I rarely even gave myself a title. "Hi, I'm Drew" always seemed to work best. Oh, and I never wore a sport coat to a business meeting again. It's safe to say I ended up taking the most opposite approach possible to my wardrobe and style.

Seemingly millions of "infomercial agencies" popped up around this time. Agencies that never did infomercials started to market themselves as "experts". Most had no clue you needed balls and some intuition. A rare combination.) Anyway, almost overnight, freshly minted "infomercial geniuses" in their cookie-cutter suits, dress shoes, and perfectly combed hair started popping up all over. And how they looked reflected the work they produced. It was generic, stale and underwhelming. (It also reflected an industry average failure rate that hovered around 80 percent. At the same time, our agency was the polar opposite, averaging around an 80 percent success rate.) I wanted to be different from these other groups in every way imaginable. So, yeah, I showed up to my meetings, shoots — anything and everything — in jeans, cowboy boots, a backwards baseball cap, and a t-shirt. I chose not to be with the sheep and never looked back.

This is also when I started going more "public" with my tattoos. We were filming a fitness infomercial for a gold medal Olympian, and I showed up at the morning workout in a tank top, revealing the tattoo on my left arm and the three on my right — all of which were usually hidden under a normal t-shirt. The Olympian was surprised and made a friendly, light-hearted comment about my tattoos, because twenty years ago, tattoos were more uncommon, especially for someone in my position.

At the time, I wasn't fully aware that I was…changing my skin, as well as my persona. Oddly, when I landed on a design for a new tattoo I wanted, I felt a weird internal drive to *get it done fast,* once I knew the piece of the puzzle I wanted to work on next. I also anticipated the next one and the next one. I didn't have a mid- or long-term concept or end goal vision. It was all very short-term and immediate. Back then, there was no Instagram or tattoo websites to find artists or help you come up with designs. Getting a tattoo was A LOT of blind luck, walking into a tattoo parlor, flipping through four or five different portfolio books, selecting an artist based on their past work, and off you went. There was no big picture creative ideation like we have today or the consciousness that some pieces would flow into others or have a big picture theme. At least not for me.

One of my first four tattoos was what some people would call a "peekaboo." Meaning, it was on the middle of my left arm, so it was *usually* covered by a shirt, BUT, if you wore a specific short sleeve shirt that shrunk or just had high-cut sleeves, the bottom of the tattoo would peek out. I stretched forward to grab a glass of water during a shoot and a client gasped, "You have tattoos!?" I became increasingly aware of the surprise and shock value even a small peekaboo brought, as well as the general perception of tattoos at the time.

I guess you could say my fifth tattoo was a milestone. It was my first tattoo (drumroll) below the elbow. The tattoo artist said, "Ya sure you're good with this placement? It's a barrier you're crossing." I never forgot that. Fuck. It felt like I was busting out of the joint or making it all the way to homebase with a girl for the first time. Barriers. Crossed. What a fucking rush. That made my heart race when he said that. In a good way. And he was NOT trying to talk me out of it. He was covered in tattoos. He was just being a good person and a responsible artist by making sure he wasn't going to put someone in a position they would later regret. I was probably very ready, because as soon as he started the tattoo, my eyes began scanning my arms for my next tattoo and where it would go. I was hooked.

For the last twenty years, I haven't been able to find my tattoo "off" button. The moment I firm up a concept and artist for a new one, I'm already anticipating four or five other new ones. I've never thought about stopping, nor have I wanted to. And unlike booze and drugs, post-tattoo you don't wake up feeling like shit the next day. In the days after a new tattoo, I actually still feel the RUSH of it.

After I got that barrier-crossing lower arm tattoo, I rode in a cab to pitch a very conservative company's HQ in a very conservative state. I wore jeans, boots, and a t-shirt, i.e., my normal uniform, but because it was a chilly day, I also wore a flannel over-shirt. I got warm right before walking into the meeting and removed the flannel. A woman traveling with me from my company saw the new lower arm tattoo and was...surprised. "Wow, that's very...*noticeable*. How do you think these people will react?" "I guess we'll find out," I laughed.

◆ ◆ ◆

I'm obsessed with realness and despise fake, staged crap with a passion. That led me to coin the tagline, "Real people, real stories, real results" twenty-plus years ago. It's since been used, reused, and copy-catted in countless campaigns for the biggest brands — many I had nothing to do with, and the same brands would have tossed an ad agency out on its ass in a split second back then if they ever pitched, "Let's be real, let's be authentic, let's actually show real humans for who they really are versus who we think they should be."

Most people recoil at the thought of an infomercial. "Fake" and "sleazy" are often attributed to them and the people who make them. But what made my productions stand out was taking the opposite approach. I rejected slick tactics and doubled down on REAL. I didn't succeed despite keeping it real, I succeeded *because* of it.

It took me three years of hustling to finally make inroads into that industry. No film school, no favors or inside contacts. Just a shit ton of relentless grinding, without ever getting sucked into conforming to what society and the industry told me was the "right" way to do things. We often underestimate how much people *don't* want convention. More often than not, we crave relief from it. The over-sized guy in cowboy boots and head-to-toe tattoos can feel like a breath of fresh air in a sea of human robots, and a 30-minute infomercial (when done right) can provide more "realness" than those sheep stuck in bubbles of conformity experience in a month.

No, I won't say your life is one long infomercial, but ask yourself: if it *were*, would you want to buy what you're selling?

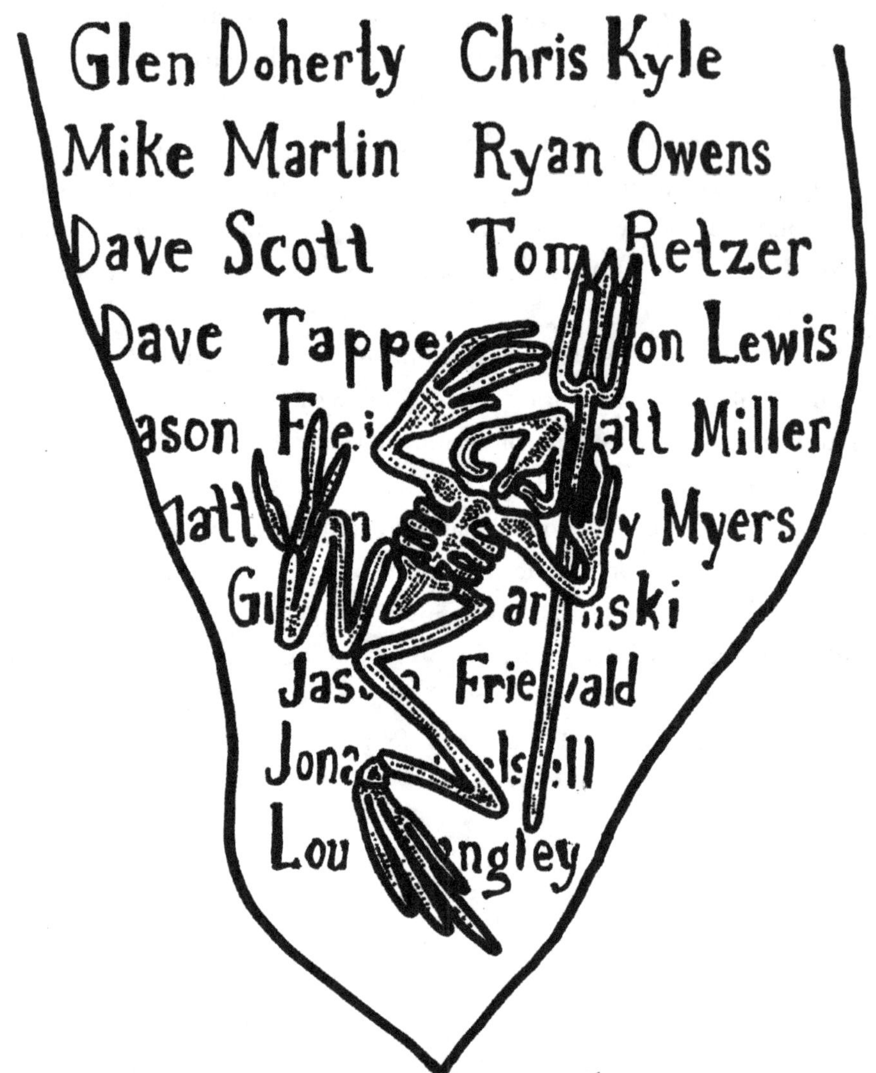

FALLEN HEROES Clint Emerson, Retired Navy Seal

Mike Martin was a legend: a Vietnam SEAL, Hell's Angel, and was tatted from the bottom of his ear, all the way to his toe. He also really liked his...cock! The first time I met him, as a new guy, I was in the shower. Imagine a guy fully tatted, butt naked, standing in front of you, with the voice and accent of Joe Pesci, talking to me with his dick touching my inner thigh.

Chris Kyle was at SEAL Team 3 with me. We were both Texas kids, and we became fast friends just because of like-minded Texas pride. We did the initial push into Iraq together. Chris was the "American Sniper," but he was just a good ol' boy. And a good friend.

Jonas Kelsall was the main officer with the Captain Phillips rescue. He was the guy who was creative enough to lure one of the Somali pirates onto the boat, separate them, and create the disgruntledness between the pirates that were on the capsule with Phillips and their leader on the boat.

Glen Doherty was almost 30 when he joined the Navy, making him one of the older guys to go through BUD/S. He'd already hitchhiked across America following the Grateful Dead, worked on an Alaskan fishing boat, then landed at a microbrewery somewhere in California. One night around a campfire, some SEALs said, "Hey man, you should join the Navy and be a SEAL!" So the next day he went and joined the Navy – and became a SEAL.

Every single person who knew Glen says, "He was my best friend." That tells you a lot. He was also the guy you loved to hate because he was fucking good at everything. No matter what you were doing, he was better. "Fuck, I hate you!" We did two deployments together, then he went to the CIA and died in Benghazi.

Seeing something physical that's permanent – like a military monument or a tattoo – it's there forever. I never want anyone to forget my buddies. I remember them for who they were, the funny stories, the shit they did, their calmness, and the crazy crap they pulled off.

Each of these guys, I either deployed with, was friends with, or went through training with. Tattoos generate conversation. Not only does it keep their memory, but – they're dead; it's really for their families. Their families want their brother, their son, and their husband's memory to stay alive. There's no better way to do it than a tattoo.

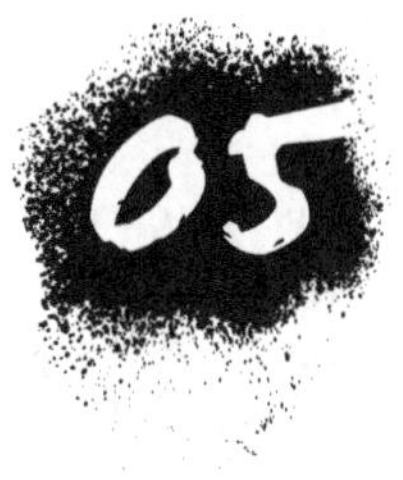

BABY MURDER IN ETHIOPIA

GETTING HIGH... (ON DISCOMFORT)

Mingi is an ancient practice where elders and parents murder babies they believe are cursed, and it still exists in some remote Ethiopian tribal villages. What makes these newborns and toddlers cursed? Any number of mundane, random, completely innocent things, like being born out of wedlock or their top teeth appearing before the bottom ones. Or being born as twins. Being "cursed" is an automatic death sentence, and a brutal death is required to properly kill the curse and protect the village: the baby might be starved, left out for wild animals, tossed in a river to drown, strangled, or suffocated, their mouth filled with dirt. It's horrific.

I first heard of mingi from a woman in California who adopted a mingi rescue baby years ago. My oldest daughter is also adopted from Ethiopia, and I feel a strong connection with that place, so in 2018, when I heard about Lale Labuko, a Kara tribesman and the superhero who rescues mingi babies, I wanted to help. I wanted to give back to the country and people who blessed me with my first child years prior.

Moody (yes, his real name), my close pal in Texas, told me about Lale and his orphanage in Ethiopia. After rescuing the condemned babies, Lale places them in his orphanage to be raised as one family. At the time, there were sixty kids living there. Lale was one of the few members of the Kara tribe to be educated outside of the village, and for him, the fight to end mingi is personal: his twin sisters were killed for being mingi. He's dedicated his life to demonstrating that the mingi children were never actually cursed, and educating the tribe about how the children saved from execution have all grown up to be healthy and successful.

Moody, an orthodontist with seven kids, including three adopted from Ethiopia, has always been the best human I know. A successful business owner and leader in his community, amazing father, husband, and true friend, as well as an incredible role model of what it means to be a "good" man, Moody is polished, professional, and patient. Basically the opposite of me. He's a khakis and wrinkle-free, tucked-in polo shirt kinda guy. And always happy. I swear this fucker must have a smile on his face when he sleeps, 'cause I can't recall ever seeing him for more than a few minutes where he wasn't smiling. His positivity beams out of his asshole like a 500-watt bulb. Then there's me — black t-shirt, sneakers, metal on my wrists (bracelets, not handcuffs, thankfully), tinted glasses always (thanks to a genuine light sensitivity issue with my eyes), huge beard, and an endless volcanic eruption of tattoos. When we're together, I look like his bodyguard. Or he looks like my parole officer.

We both always felt drawn to give back to Ethiopia for giving us our kids. Ethiopia was one of the countries where my non-profit, Global Mobility, brought free wheelchairs, and Moody started a free dental clinic there called Ethiopia Smiles. So when he said Lale needed support to save more babies from being sentenced to death, it was oddly very natural for us to just fly there and see what we could do to help. Some dudes road trip to Vegas for a wild time. Moody and I set out for one of the more remote and potentially deadly areas imaginable.

My biggest fear centered on the challenges of getting to and from this exceptionally remote village. After flying from Los Angeles to Ethiopia, followed by another in-country flight, and many more hours on 3rd world roads, the closest town to the actual tribal village was still several hours away, sitting somewhere on a deserted dirt road in the middle of absolutely fucking nowhere. (Seriously…if Waze actually worked there, I'm guessing it would say "middle of fucking nowhere" as the destination.) We had a few concerns, as you might imagine. What if our truck broke down? Plus, as we crossed a riverbed with flowing water that almost swept us away, our driver casually said, "I hope it does not rain before we come back this way to get home." "Is that a big deal?" I asked. "No," he replied, "We just wait a month or two until the river goes down and we can pass again." Not the response I was hoping for. (Plus, with no cell phone signals, it occurred to me we could go missing for months with no one knowing what happened to us. *Holy. Shit.*) Thankfully, we managed to push the truck to safety in knee-deep water across the riverbed.

On the drive to and from the village, when not contemplating the possibility of being stuck camping by the dusty riverbanks for months, I also worried about very realistic hostile scenarios. We were right on the border of Kenya, Ethiopia, and Sudan. There are no border signs. None. No roads. No nothing. Only days earlier, two Cuban medical workers were kidnapped and executed in this exact area for providing medical aid to Kenyans. Turns out the Sudanese rebels didn't appreciate the aid workers helping their Kenyan enemies, so they sent a message by killing the doctors. (That's why I kept calling my friend DOCTOR Moody. "Hey DOCTOR Moody! How's it going up there?" To make it clear just who the doctor was…)

Now even though we had zero intention or desire to cross the border, it was impossible to know where the fuck it was! There was just dirt and rock in every direction. If Sudanese rebels drove up and attacked us, who was going to stop them? The closest thing we had to a powerful weapon at that point was the smell from my underarms after almost three days without a shower. No one was regulating whether we were technically in Ethiopia or Kenya or if we'd drifted over to Sudan. There were no police, no military. They could have killed us just to take the truck we were in. Or used us as free target practice. We were in a lawless, unmarked area, and completely at the mercy of the locals we might encounter, our fate decided by people who may or may not want to make an example of a heavily tattooed, goofy-looking bastard with ripe pits, who had no good explanation for what the fuck he was doing there.

Lale told us that the week before we arrived, two more children were murdered for mingi. I thought of that often on the journey to the village. Especially me being the father of twin girls back home, who in this tribal village, would be considered, mingi. To this day, I wonder: Would things have been different for the tribe's most recent murdered babies had we gotten there a week sooner? Planned our trip just seven days earlier? Who knows. But the thought stays with me.

Finally, after several hours of unpleasant "what if?" imaginings while off-roading through the wide open unknown, we approached the village. The men all carried AK-47 rifles and machetes; the women mostly had babies attached to their breasts or strapped to their backs — or both — with smaller kids trailing behind them. Ethiopians in general are very small, so someone my size was very... unusual. Plus, I was white and covered in tattoos. The villagers walked up to me and started touching my arms, running their fingers over my tattoos with a soft cooing sound, entranced.

They introduced me to the main warrior of the village, who was branded with scars (their version of tattoos) all over his body. Each scar represented a time he killed someone to protect the village. The assumption was I had done something comparable to "earn" my markings. (This is where Dr. Moody told the heavily tattooed warrior that, because I had tattoos, I wanted to challenge him to battle. Clearly payback for calling him *DOCTOR* MOODY loudly on our journey.)

Lale served as our guide and translator and introduced us to the villagers and chief. He warned us: this was *not* a casual social visit. If the chief did not bless our visit — for any reason — we needed to leave. FAST. There were no legal authorities or military, no running water, not even the concept of time. It was like I had stepped into the pages of *National Geographic*, XXX edition, where every moment is a question of life or death. I tried to get some clarity around what would determine whether the chief would bless us or if we should run for the potentially overflowing riverbed, but no one offered any definitive answer. I guess it depended on his mood. Great.

To this day, I think the chief blessed us and let us stay because of one thing: My big, fat ass.

All the men in the village carve their own little stools, which they carry around: rifle over one arm, machete across their backs, and tiny stool hanging from their waists. They use the stools as seats at their meetings with the other men. Sitting in the men's circle is a sign of manhood, but it must be earned (in part by running on the backs of bulls without falling).

As visitors, we were to sit in the men's circle on the provided "visitors' stools," surrounded by our heavily armed, trigger-happy hosts, who kept firing their weapons into the air to honor the dead. (How long had they been dead? No one knew. Remember, the tribe did not keep or track 'time'.)

Lale explained that the chief was assessing if he felt we were good, and therefore deserving of a blessing, or evil — and had to go…fast.

So, the stools. Did I mention they were really fucking small? I'm 6'4, 240 pounds. Moody is much smaller and managed to sit on his little stool fine. Lil' cramped, but he handled it like a champ. (Show off). Me? Not so much. Truthfully, I could not even FEEL the wood under my ass. I've drunk out of beer mugs that were bigger. I tried to visualize it — like a golf putt or something requiring focus. And when I finally felt the tiny piece of wood beneath me, I decided to take my shot and…sit.

Not even close.

I rolled backward in the dirt and almost flipped over. Then again. And again. One failed attempt to sit after another. After my fourth roll, the men broke their serious stares. They could no longer cover their smiles. All at once, they roared with laughter. And then the chief smiled and overflowed into hysterical laughter. Lale said he had never seen this before; laughing was not a common part of their culture.

Moments later, the chief blessed our visit and invited us to stay. (Whew, my balls could stop sweating.) He said some words — a prayer, a chant — but whatever it was, it meant we were IN.

We shared with them that we each had children born in Ethiopia. Beautiful, magical babies that were growing into wonderful humans in California and Texas.

All because a brave birth parent in Ethiopia chose to bless them and us with a happy life together as a family. We showed them photos of our Ethiopian kids on our phones, and we asked if they would consider blessing more babies and new mommies and daddies by letting the children live safely and happily at Lale's orphanage, or even join new families in Ethiopia. We assured them the babies would leave the village and take the curse with them. Everybody wins! That was the idea at least.

One of the most profound moments of the trip was not at the village, but the mingi orphanage. Our last night there, the kids held a special dinner for us. Some could speak a little English, others used a translator. Two of the older girls wanted to become doctors. They both were on track to get scholarships to medical school. The vast majority of Ethiopians who do become doctors practice in America or Europe to escape the poverty. I assumed these kids would be especially eager to escape the memory of parents who believed they were cursed and wanted them dead. But no. These young girls, each around fourteen years old, had far different goals and dreams. They wanted to practice medicine a few hours up the dirt road from the orphanage, right back at their home village. They wanted to go back and provide medical care for the same village that sentenced them to death, simply because their teeth came in top down versus bottom up. Their reason? "They are our family. We love them. They had no education and did not understand that mingi is wrong. If we can provide medicine and education and love, THAT is how no more babies will be killed anymore for mingi."

The words from those two girls still fucking rock me to this day and always will. I think of it so often. It speaks to a deep, profound selflessness that is so rare; it may as well be extinct. These girls, on track to become doctors, could get rich (insanely rich, by local standards) and live safe, secure lives abroad, far from the village that condemned them to death. And yet, these young girls had zero anger at their parents or village for trying to kill them. They simply accept it as ignorance — a failure of education. I would refer to these young ladies as heroic, but that word doesn't do justice to what they truly are. It's unclear whether they would even be allowed back at the village or if they'd be killed trying, but they were very clear in their hearts' desire to return.

The hardest thing to explain about my experience was how everyone's actions, as misguided and even fucked up as they surely are (killing babies!), was genuinely rooted in…love. The villagers truly love their children and each other. They are ready and willing to die for the good of the village as a whole, and they believe with all their hearts that killing a few of their own children will stop the curse, which in turn saves tens of thousands of lives. They don't murder them out of evil or anger, but out of superstition. Yes, it is archaic, but they only know what they know, what has been passed down for centuries.

Love was also the dominant emotion at the orphanage — a very modest house, with Lale and a few "house mamas" raising over sixty children, all of whom narrowly escaped death. All of them sentenced to die at the hands of their own families. Love was the currency exchanged in their "palace." Each mingi orphan did not lose a family; they became part of a much bigger one, complete with sixty brothers and sisters, Lale is their father, and the army of women who cook, clean, and love the children as their own mother them. Lale reminds them daily they are blessings, not curses.

We returned from the village hopeful our pleas and ideas (and offers of medical supplies and future support) were heard and would make a difference. I can't say for sure if our efforts that day saved any babies directly. Maybe. Maybe not. "Progress" in those villages does not take place in the way or on the timeline we Westerners might want. Sometimes a meeting like ours impacts the chief's decision in a day, a week, or even months later. So the reality is, after we left, more babies were killed, and more babies were saved by Lale and sent to live in the orphanage. But to this day and forever on, the entire experience reminds me of the power of getting off your ass and being willing to get uncomfortable and take risks if you want to make any type of meaningful change.

I have an ongoing goal to get away from…normal. I don't like normal. It's a mind-numbingly boring and dreary way to go through life. Tens of millions of people go to Disneyland every year. And the Eiffel tower and Buckingham Palace. How many outsiders visit this Ethiopian tribe?

My professional career has been full of getting uncomfortable and pushing myself into the unknown. One of the first commercials I ever directed was for Paris Hilton. Leading up to the shoot, I kept thinking I'd get the call any minute saying they'd made a mistake and never meant to hire ME. But somehow that call didn't come, and I was on my way.

Experts say homo sapiens emerged around 300,000 years ago. But it wasn't until very (very) recently that humans learned the concept of "comfort." We were explorers who hunted and died. By nature, we are survivalists. I believe that natural instinct still flows through our veins, which is why many of us feel discontent sitting still behind desks, driving in cars, and being tethered to endless phone calls and Zooms. Being uncomfortable isn't weird or sadistic. It's intuitive to our evolution. It's human nature.

Uncomfortable situations make me feel more alive. More present. As a teenager, I can't say I wasn't a bit nervous visiting death row, surrounded by 600 condemned dudes in cages on either side of me. But it's these *where the fuck am I?* situations that force you to grow and evolve, by testing your limits and pushing past them.

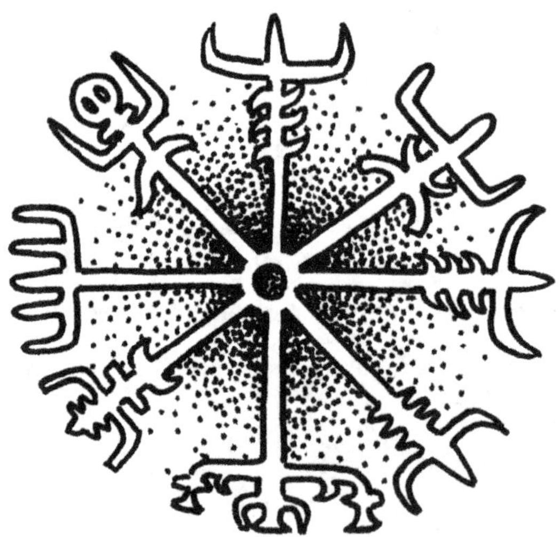

Whenever I venture into these off-grid foreign places, physically or mentally, I think of the round shield tattooed on my right shoulder. On it is a vegvísir, an Icelandic symbol intended to protect the bearer in rough weather. It's also a compass (vegvísir means "that which shows the way"). It guides me through the rough seas and strong headwinds of life, even when I have no fucking idea where I'm going. While I don't follow any particular faith exclusively, I very much believe in God, which is why I like focusing some of my tattoos on symbolism that calls for protection from a higher power. I do a lot of stupid shit, so it's nice to feel I'm being looked after "from above."

Protection does not eliminate all fears. My only real "fear" in life pertains to my kids: Will they be ok if something happens to me? In my (admittedly crazy) trip to Ethiopia, I was less worried about the chief and his blessing than an accident involving one of the young tribesmen with guns. The guns were old, unlikely ever cleaned, and full of dirt and rust. Whenever one of them started firing shots into the air, I definitely had a near change of underwear moment. These dudes definitely didn't get the safety memo about not swinging the muzzle in front of people and walking around with their fingers on the trigger. So it wasn't the safest environment on many levels — something I worry about not for me, but my kids.

I try to balance those risks with the value of living as fully as possible. Life comes down to choices: Do you choose to risk being in-over-your-head? Or do you turn back and retreat, not knowing what you may have discovered or achieved with just a few more steps? Do you seek adventure and the unknown — or comfort and safety? Your answer says a lot about who you are and what you can be. Comfort can often come at the expense of experience, knowledge, exploration. I often choose to live in discomfort. Maybe it's literal, leading you to remote parts of the globe. Or maybe it's internal, pushing you to explore ideas and emotions that make you want to hit the eject button immediately. It's like the Jerry Rice quote that's become the sports training mantra: "Today I will do what others won't, so tomorrow I can do what others can't." Only, too often we excuse what we *don't* do as what we "can't" do. There's a lot that I try to do, only to crash and burn. But, if given a choice, I always choose discomfort over living half-way.

Meeting Lale made me a better person, a better father, a better everything. More patient, more thankful, less greedy. The young girls who want to go back and practice medicine amongst the people who tried to murder them helped me to reframe other situations in my own life and be more generous in how I read and reacted to them. And every child we ever fitted with a wheelchair who thanked me, smiled, gave me the best hugs of my life, and wheeled away so happy — even though I wanted to cry my fucking eyes out cause these lil' kids would still never walk again, would likely never have access to proper medical care — made me more grateful and humble than any tattoo can adequately capture.

The most uncomfortable experiences of my life have been my greatest teachers.

I've lived fully. And yet, the wildest party, best mushroom trip, and greatest thrill-seeking getaway combined never came close to the high I feel in moments when I can truly be of service. Especially when it's for a total stranger who can never possibly repay you. It is the ultimate high.

Whenever I find myself getting too comfortable, I'm usually being lazy. Complacent. Selfish. Gluttonous. And the only solution is to get uncomfortable, *again*. It's my drug of choice. It's my addiction.

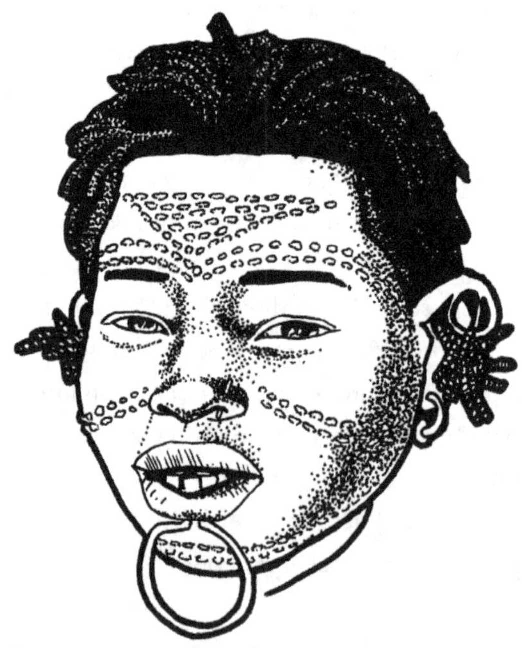

Ethiopian girls mark their bodies with scars as a symbol of beauty and bravery.

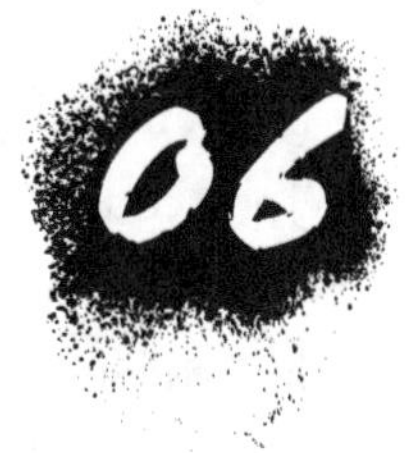

SAINTS, SINNERS, AND SPRINGSTEEN

FINDING MY RELIGION

I was NOT a fan of Springsteen growing up. No way, man. I was an 80s kid in New Jersey! That meant glam/hair metal and heavy metal bands (Poison, Britny Fox, Cinderella, Bon Jovi, Mötley Crüe, and of course, Metallica). Not sure I even knew who Springsteen was back then. We weren't exactly musically "well-rounded." Nobody who was into metal would be suicidal enough to also share how much they enjoyed…Huey Lewis and the News or…Springsteen, for that matter. They were in different solar systems. The ONLY music that existed in my small lil' ink splatter of a world was LOUD metal and BIG HAIR bands. I played drums around that time, and most local ads for a drummer / singer / guitar player would literally start out with: "BIG HAIR/GREAT HAIR A MUST." That's right, before mentioning a word about musical skills, it was about the HAIR.

So, in reality, even though I was born in Springsteen's hometown of Freehold, NJ, he could have walked right past me and I would have had zero clue who he was. But anytime an anorexic, wafer-thin dude in black spandex pants (usually adorned with some variety of metal studs or chains) and massive hair walked by, it was…FUCKING EPIC.

I was twelve years old when the *Born in the U.S.A.* album was released. It took Springsteen from big to MEGA HUUUUGE. So there was no way to avoid hearing some of his hits on the radio, especially with my summers spent down at the Jersey Shore. I remember my older brother and cousins talking about Springsteen, but I would roll my eyes and mouth-off about Metallica, Def Leppard, or Quiet Riot. (I mean seriously, our sixth-grade kickball team was named The Quiet Riots!)

After I graduated from ASU, I did a few cross-country drives with my best friend, Terry. We each drove our own cars in a mini two-car convoy from Arizona or Utah, where he lived, to New Jersey, then back out West again. We repeated this trip three or four times. That's A LOT of alone time in a car (especially pre-audiobooks / Spotify / satellite radio / podcasts). The FM radio and my own thoughts were my only companions for thousands of miles of black-top.

I knew my musical tastes were…due for expansion, so when something other than my usual music came on a station, I tried to listen. Sometime around hour 'who-the-fuck-knows' on the open road, I realized I was pausing on a lot of songs from the same person: Springsteen. Many of his songs were oddly familiar; I just hadn't realized they were his.

At the time, I didn't know much about him other than he was also from New Jersey. But during those isolated drives, his music and lyrics…they started to call me in. They spoke to me. He was singing about…my struggles, my dreams, my journey. Each track was less of a song and more of a story. Not just any story but a parable, a life lesson or experience set to music. Unlike most other radio hits back then, his songs weren't 3.5 minute soulless commercial tunes. Some of his were over ten minutes long! He didn't seem as concerned with finding a catchy hook so much as telling a great fucking story. And then — right in the middle of the songs — this dude would stop singing and *speak*. To the audience, to me, about his ghosts, his angels, his demons. He shared stories of his life — the good, the bad, and the really fucking ugly. I had never heard a rockstar talk about anything other than how great the drugs were and how hot the chicks were. But THIS dude was…authentic. In a way I had never experienced. And he sang about places I knew. Places I'd heard of and many I had experienced first-hand. Places that played a meaningful part in my own life. Then…WAIT — I realized he was actually from Freehold, New Jersey. The same forgettable lil' town where I was born. Imagine that. This guy WAS talking to me. He *knew* me. And I felt like I knew him.

When I was in Reno chasing TV news, it was a lonely ass time. So I listened to a lot of music and read books (you know, what people did pre-internet, pre-cell phones and streaming services). I also started buying older Springsteen albums, CDs and some bootleg VHS tapes. Not just the new hits currently playing on the radio, but his full catalog. Man, this dude had HISTORY. And passion. He played concerts for four fucking hours! Most artists at the time played forty-five-minute shows and headed for the door.

I connected with so many of his lyrics, but there was one subject that grabbed me the most: He talked a lot about his father. A lot. It was a complicated relationship. But the details, they sounded…familiar. Like chills-on-arms familiar. After a while, I joked to myself, "Fucking Springsteen stole my life story and shared it with the world." Except for the fact that he was a rockstar, and I couldn't sing a note or play a chord. But all the personal stuff? From his birthplace to his family dynamics to his internal struggles — it all felt like looking in the mirror. It was part music plus part therapy and it combined to fill a needy gap in my soul.

I guess that was the genesis of what became a lifelong "relationship" with The Boss. People joke about fans who are obsessed with rock stars, well my Springsteen fixation grew so intense I was (jokingly) referred to as a "stalker" by *60 Minutes*. (I was in Kilkenny, Ireland, at one of his shows, standing right up front by the stage, an American flag in one hand and a sign in the other that read, "I'm from Freehold, NJ!" Though, in my defense, he did point at me multiple times during the show.)

The truth is, it's never been a stalker-type obsession. I've never waited outside hotel rooms or made any real effort to meet him in person. Probably because, in some ways, I feel like I *have* met him, through the similar roads our lives have traveled, growing up in small town New Jersey, and the similar dynamics of a strained father/son relationship.

It'll therefore come as no surprise to learn that I have two different Springsteen-related tattoos. One of them is on my shoulder and says "Saints and Sinners." It's from the chorus of a song called "Land of Hopes and Dreams."

I've always been drawn to irony and dichotomy. I believe we are all pulled in opposite directions internally — like opposing magnets that repel, rather than draw together. It's an innate human struggle. We are all very much saints and sinners. I don't say this in a biblical sense — I'm in no position to be a valid source of biblical content or meaning, but that simultaneous pull to be both a saint and a sinner — man, it's human fucking nature to its core. It's why we use phrases like "brings out the best and worst in us." Springsteen often refers to "our better angels" and "our darker angels," and I have long recognized how both of those forces spar and kick the living shit out of each other within me.

To be clear, I don't believe I am anything close to a saint. I tend to have inner desires that probably most often land in the "selfish" bucket, while my "selfless" bucket sits way too empty by my metrics. My personal acknowledgment of this inherent flaw is what often compels me to outwardly behave in a non-selfish way (some formal public "giving back" and a bunch of "anonymous" stuff that will remain that way). On my torso is a tattoo in Spanish of Matthew 20:16, *The last shall be the first and the first shall be the last.* That is my way of reminding myself to do the right fucking thing — otherwise *I might not remember.* Because it doesn't always come naturally.

My outward acts of selflessness are, of course, the visible and obvious ones the world sees. People comment, "You are wonderful for doing this!" or "You're so amazing for doing that!" And those comments make me want to crawl out of my skin. I try to shut them down. I actually look away, look down, or even interrupt and change the topic. Because I know, no matter what we do externally, most of us, deep inside, can be very ugly. And I'm no exception.

I'm not speaking about evil desires of hurting people or other sadistic urges. I just mean sins like material desire, jealousy, vanity — things like that. And in many ways, a lot of my outward acts are my way of repenting or making up for my internal flaws that are not as "pure" or genuine as I might hope. I guess it's a sort of "Catholic guilt" for a non-Catholic.

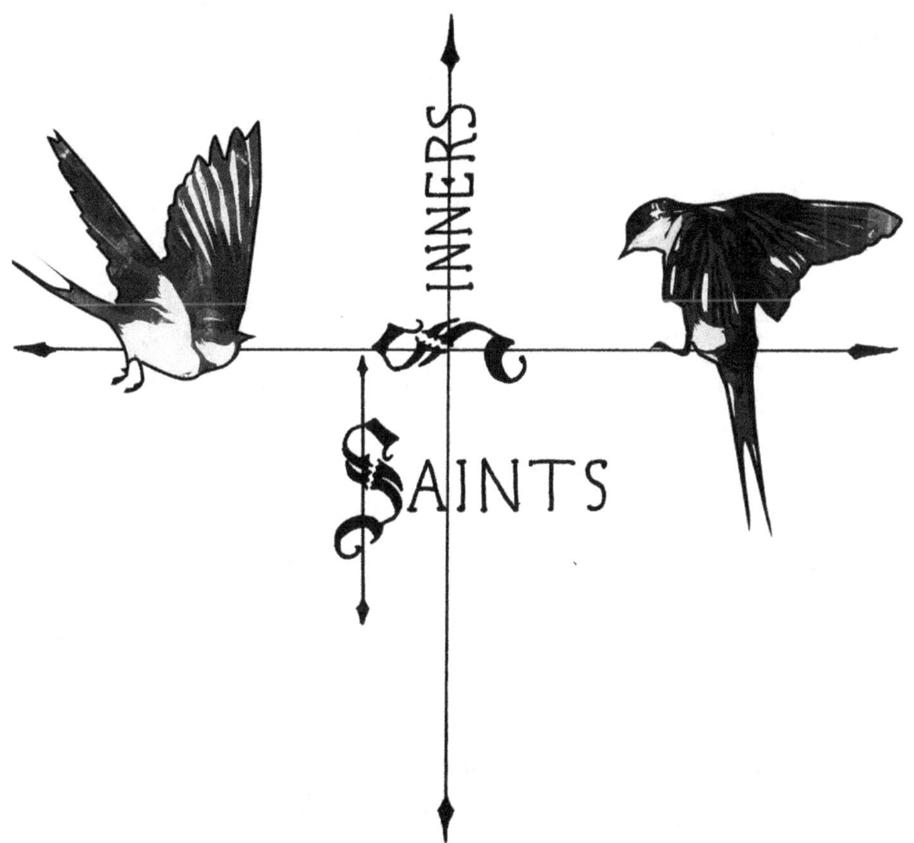

So the "Saints and Sinners" tattoo reflects my own internal struggle with both my better angels and my darker angels — and yeah, those two fuckers BRAWL inside of me, like an MMA championship bloodbath that never ends.

While Springsteen's words were my inspiration, I added some imagery to the design to personalize it: A compass, symbolizing my perpetually changing direction. Internally, I've never found "home." Then a picture of a bird that stays put and another raising its wings, ready to bolt at any moment. That's me my entire life: One foot in and one foot out. I'll stay planted for months, years, decades…but am ready to bolt every second of those years on end. Inside I just want to "hop aboard the train of saints and sinners" and roll away. Destination unknown.

Finding Springsteen wasn't a cool music discovery, it was — as weird as it sounds — part of my path to self-discovery. Part of my never-ending journey to understanding myself. Listening to his music is where I frequently find safe harbor from the rogue waves in my darkest storms.

Springsteen played on Broadway a few years ago, and it was pretty epic. The guy who sold out stadiums and played concerts for over 100,000 fans, played in front of 900 people in a tiny Broadway theater. It wasn't a STAND AND SING AND ROCK OUT kinda show. It was Bruce's own telling of his journey in life, told through his music, but also his stories.

From the front row, about ten feet from the man whose personal journey so closely mirrored my own, he sang "My Father's House." It was one of several songs he wrote about his father and the challenges of their relationship, from youth to death and everything in between. In the middle of that song, at this Broadway show, he stopped singing and shared these words:

Those whose love we wanted but didn't get — we emulate them. That's the only way we had, in our power, to get the closeness and the love that we needed and desired. So when I was a young man and looking for a voice to meld with mine, to sing my songs and to tell my stories — well, I chose my father's voice. Because there was something sacred in it to me. And when I went looking for something to wear, I put on a factory worker's clothes, because they were my dad's clothes. And all we know about manhood is what we have seen and what we have learned from our fathers, and my father was my hero. And my greatest foe.

"My father was my hero. And my greatest foe." The thing about a true poet-philosopher, especially one who shares a freakishly similar life story, is they are able to use words to explain and communicate things that live inside you. Feelings, unresolved emotions, raw pain points. It's like an unsolved crossword puzzle that is 100% fucking maddening and 0% fun. But that rare lyrical genius is able to unlock the mystery and link words with emotions. When someone else is able to use *their* words to connect the dots and say the things *you* feel and lived — but which you couldn't articulate, even to yourself — that's a musically religious experience. It's that "Yeah, what he said" feeling. And for some odd reason, hearing him say those words made me feel more understood…to *me*…to myself. And that was something, at least.

Later in the set, he sang another song called "Long Time Coming." The lyrics to that song always reminded me of my own experience with my father.

Once again, as if peering into my soul, Springsteen said what I couldn't, just before singing that song:

Here in the last days before I was to become a father, my own father was visiting me to warn me of the mistakes that he had made, and to warn me not to make them with my own children. To release them from the chain of our sins, my father of mine and our fathers before, that they may be free, to make their own choices and to live their own lives. We are ghosts or we are ancestors in our children's lives. We either lay our mistakes, our burdens, upon them, and we haunt them, or we assist them in laying those old burdens down, and we free them from the chain of our own flawed behavior. And as ancestors, we walk alongside them, and we assist them in finding their own way, and some transcendence.

My father, on that day, was petitioning me for an ancestral role in my life, after being a ghost for a long, long time. He wanted me to write a new end to our relationship, and he wanted me to be ready for the new beginning that I was about to experience. It was the greatest moment in my life with my dad, and it was all that I needed.

Those words reverberated: "Writing a new end to our relationship…it was all I ever needed."

I want to say I was happy for Springsteen, this man whose music and words had given me so much — a soundtrack for my life, lyrical guidance, relatable wisdom. But the truth is, I was pretty wounded. Not by Bruce directly, per se. But that he confirmed one of the most painful realities in my life — one I already knew, but tried to ignore, deny, and hide from: There would never be a happy ending or any kind of meaningful closure between my father and me. Our lives were so parallel, and yet, I knew that cinematic scene Springsteen experienced with his father was never gonna happen for me.

Springsteen has no tattoos.

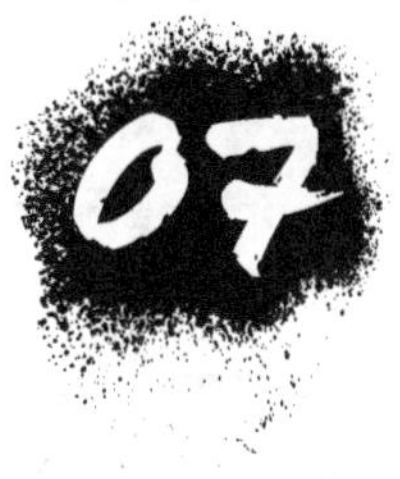

MY FATHER

HERO AND FOE

June 9, 2018 was one of those perfect SoCal days — the kind we take pictures of and send to our friends back East to justify the hefty price tag and other BS we put up with for our geographic life choice. I spent the day at the beach with my kids, but despite the external perfection — the sun on my face, my happy laughing Irish triplets, aka my littles — I felt this weird inner pull all day. It wasn't a normal sensation; nothing familiar. Not a solid kick in the balls, but definitely far from anything remotely comforting or good. Watching my kids run through the waves without a care in the world, I grew increasingly agitated and restless. I was coming out of my skin. Without reason. (Or so I thought.)

Chef-turned-traveling storyteller Anthony Bourdain died by suicide the day before, and it weighed heavily on me. Far more than I'd anticipated when I heard the tragic news. I'm not a big Facebook guy and rarely post anything serious, but I'd seen several posts from some couch ninjas who were "angry" at him for taking his own life. And it didn't sit well with me. It actually pissed me off.

I don't watch much TV, but I devoured Bourdain's show. Eating, boozing, dropping F-bombs — we bonded through the screen. I made my career with big crews, large sets, huge lights / gear / tech, and an entourage of makeup folks (the "pretty committee"), and certain oversized celebrity egos that in some cases were larger than the production itself. Bourdain, on the other hand, operated lean and light. He was a minimalist who understood the value of authenticity and keeping it real. He knew life wasn't perfect, and that's what made his show "perfect."

Like me, Bourdain also felt uncomfortable in his own skin. Early on, the producers had serious doubts about the viability of his show because he was so visibly uncomfortable on camera. But that's exactly what made all of us so *comfortable* watching him. He was relatable and authentic. Plus, the brilliant bastard was from the Great Nation of New Jersey. What's not to like?

So when this man I admired through the screen exited for good and so unexpectedly, I was incredibly saddened. And the way we lost him hit a little too close to home.

My father never apologized to me for trying to take his life all those years back when I was thirteen. As a father now, I can't imagine deliberately doing anything that would cause my kids pain. And if I were to hurt them, I would do anything in my power to make it right — to reassure them that whatever hurt I caused was about me, not them. I would hate for them to wonder or live without that reassurance.

I think, at times, my father had a genuine desire to make things right with the past, with me. Especially in the years right after his first suicide attempt. But he had a limited capacity to address it. His darker angels would get the best of his better angels on this topic. Always.

When I heard about Bourdain's suicide, it triggered something in me. Maybe I still needed closure from all those decades prior. Or maybe I was just fucking heartbroken to lose someone I never met, but somehow felt so damn connected to? Regardless, I knew I had a therapeutic need to speak up to the social media trolls attacking him in death.

The idea that "forgiveness is a gift you give yourself" repeated in my head as I tapped out my Facebook post:

I find Anthony Bourdain's passing as sad as most others do. And while I understand some people being so sad and hurt that they express 'anger' or 'blame' toward him for his actions, I simply feel those sentiments are misguided and unfortunate. He was clearly in such severe pain, he made a choice that is far more severe than many of us can imagine. And as sad as his departure from this world is, it is equally sad that countless others whose names we don't know have also departed in the same tragic, pain-ridden manner.

Personally, I believe to be angry or point fingers at Anthony Bourdain or anyone who ends their pain in this manner is no different than being critical of someone who died of lung cancer after being a smoker. Or being angry and critical of someone for 'working too hard' after they died of a heart attack. Or blaming someone who died from liver failure because they drank too much. I would no sooner speak ill of someone for speeding who died in a car wreck than I would of someone who opted to take their own life via suicide.

Death is not the time to point fingers and second guess. Far from it. In reality, my heart breaks perhaps a bit more for someone who takes their own life intentionally. It suggests their pain was likely constant, severe, and fairly well-hidden in most cases.

I'm sure heaven is alive tonight with quite the tasting menu. Farewell, Chef. Thanks for the memories and for reminding us to enjoy the things we often take for granted.

Shared with Your friends 👥 *June 9, 2018*

I knew the words of forgiveness I was writing were a gift to myself and no one else. Reflecting on the suicide of a man I'd never met was my way — the only way I knew how — of forgiving my father for what he'd attempted all those years ago, and for the painful burden he'd unknowingly given me to carry ever since. I didn't mention my father's suicide attempt in the post. We were always raised to conceal what would have been considered a huge embarrassment, so I kept that secret hidden inside my entire life, along with my hurt, anger, and confusion.

I hadn't actually spoken to my father in several years leading up to the day after Bourdain's death when I made the above Facebook post. His temper and outlook on almost everything had grown very dark, and most of our attempted discussions ended abruptly. I also had a very young family and was sensitive to exposing my own kids to certain behaviors I'd lived through. His F-bombs made me sound like the Pope (not an easy feat). His political opinions had no party affiliation other than "Fuck 'em all." As a kid, he was the strongest, most powerful man in the world to me; someone I looked up to so high my neck would strain. But he had become…angry, pissed, and seemingly eager (and in his own mind, fully prepared) to deliver a first-class ass whooping with his cane to anyone who disagreed with him. There was no self-censoring, no on/off switch with him. So, sadly, we became estranged.

My father never asked for forgiveness — that wasn't really his way. But by articulating my own forgiveness of Bourdain, even via a simple public social media post, I was also, in my own way, absolving my father and giving myself the gift of relief, peace, and acceptance. I could release the baggage. It was time to finally cut the chains and move the fuck on.

The moment I posted it, it felt like a weight lifted from my heart. My soul and spirit felt freer. I was actually fucking lighter, free from decades of needing to puke, but not being able to.

No more than two minutes later, I got an urgent text from my cousin.

"Drew, call me. You need to call me."

I didn't know what she was talking about. I picked up the phone.

She said she was so sorry about my father. I had no idea what she was talking about.

"But you just posted about Anthony Bourdain. I assumed that's because of your father and what happened?"

"What happened to my father? Is he ok?"

"Oh my god. You don't know," she said quietly.

I paused. And then it hit me.

"How did he do it this time? Sounds like he was successful this time?"

My cousin burst into uncontrollable tears on the other end of the line.

I always knew this was how the story would end. I just didn't know when. I felt badly for my cousin — to be burdened with delivering such messy news to me.

"I'm so sorry that you're the one to have to make this call."

She kept sobbing. "Don't apologize to me."

I didn't allow the full reality of the news to hit me immediately. I had reluctantly prepared for this moment in my head for much of my life. Looking back, I imagine doing so was a defense mechanism to protect myself from ever experiencing (again) the shock and pain of being confronted with this type of situation. I also didn't want my own children to see the darkness I'd spent decades hiding.

The thing that pained me the most was my lack of tears. Because I had none. Not a single drop. This saddened me greatly back then and is something that has haunted me since. It's something I still try to come to terms with today, rather unsuccessfully. It wasn't because I didn't care or wasn't internally aware of the severity of what happened…the finality…the gruesome, uneditable ending — I was. But I had spent so many fucking years conditioning myself to be prepared for this that…*I was.* I was very prepared, goddamn it. I was almost robotically prepared from years of being deliberately dead inside, readying myself for the inevitable. Saying that pains me to this day. I imagine it always will.

Still dry-eyed, I went down to a local watering hole by the beach at sunset, got a few tequilas, put on my earphones, and played Springsteen's "Independence Day" on repeat. At least 100 times in a row. The song is his reflection on his own fucked up relationship with his father. Like mine, his father (as he would say) was both his greatest hero and his biggest foe. My dad inspired me as much as he enraged me. And even when I knew he could no longer be part of my life, I still somehow wanted to make him proud of who I had become and what I had accomplished.

I'm sure he felt betrayed by me. I'd abandoned him, in his mind. Stubbornness can be a good thing or a bad thing. It just depends on who writes the history. We were both stubborn. Both fighting for things we felt we could not give up or stand down from. Sometimes, despite well-intentioned negotiations and truce efforts, a war still happens. Countries and neighbors, fathers and sons. There's a fatal spark, and everything goes to total fuckville fast and furious. And once the war starts to get bloody and messy between two "superpowers," it's a hard, ugly mess to clean up and try to play nice together in the sandbox again.

Nothing with us was ever simple. Always layers of complexity and unresolved history. Most of the biggest choices we make in life will never be "good/bad" or "hard/easy" decisions. When our options are good or bad, it's not even a decision, per se. We are programmed through evolution and biology to be on autopilot and make the obvious "good" or easy decision and just keep rolling, without looking up. But in real-world reality, the decisions we are often forced to make — the ones with the most riding on them — are almost always decisions between "shitty" and "even shittier." That's where I landed with my father. There were never any easy, good/bad no-brainer decisions without consequence. And I knew we'd reached a point where lines in the sand had to be drawn and held.

While I never doubted cutting off ties in the years leading up to his death, a day never goes by that it doesn't pain me greatly. It did before his death and it does now. I had to choose between shitty and shittier, and both would haunt me. But I also know that *not* making any choice — which is especially tempting in these impossible situations — is a choice in itself.

I made the right shitty decision.

More than a few times, I've asked myself: *Am I any different than him?*

Once again, Springsteen, speaks to me:

> *My father's house shines hard and bright*
> *It stands like a beacon calling me in the night*
> *Calling and calling so cold and alone*
> *Shining 'cross this dark highway where our sins lie unatoned*

The police estimated the time of my father's death to be within a few minutes of my Facebook post. He didn't have Facebook, nor did he even know who Anthony Bourdain was. (Or Kate Spade, who hanged herself two days prior.) The timing was just a cosmic kick-in-the-balls type of thing, I suppose.

No one gets perfect parents. Some of us are lucky just to have two. Or one. Regardless of how many we get, they fail us in all sorts of ways. Often they aren't everything we'd like them to be. And I'm sure my father wouldn't have checked the box that said "heavily tattooed, sarcastic, Hollywood producer" if he had the choice between me and a future Super Bowl QB for a son. But losing a parent, especially when you're estranged and regardless of their shortcomings or your own, is difficult. It guts you.

It's impossible to avoid the tragedy of opportunity lost...or squandered. (Or both.) Some of the hardest battles we fight in life — sports, business, relationships — come down to the last two minutes on the clock. Two football teams can grind, pound, and crash into each other for four full quarters. The game may be tied, only to have one team score in the closing seconds. No matter how similar their paths, those final moments define what they remember forever — the "truth" that they carry to their graves.

Had my father not killed himself, and instead, we met for beers one day and reconciled, before he eventually died of a heart attack or a freak accident or old age, our story would have a drastically different ending. But the way those final minutes played out will forever alter the way I look at the entirety of our relationship.

You get the parents you're dealt. So, often, when someone exits under exceptionally difficult circumstances, you don't just mourn the parent you lost; you mourn the history that will never exist.

A few years after my father's death, I got a tattoo of Anthony Bourdain on my leg. He isn't smiling exactly, but he also isn't frowning. The world has not beat him. He's confident, but not exuberant. In the tattoo, I'm climbing a ladder to reach him, and I spray paint a happy smile on his cheek. That's how I think of both Bourdain and my dad. They both deserve to go out that way.

I've also added a couple more tattoos that symbolize my father to me in ways no one else would recognize. It is my way of not lying to myself or hiding the truth from myself anymore. From the age of thirteen, I hid it all. I never told a single person about what happened, because of the stigma of suicide and the unfortunate shame society dumps on those left behind. In my case, it was just understood it was never to be brought up or discussed in any circumstance. We never even talked about it within the family. It was like we were all supposed to pretend it never happened.

One day, when my father and I went fishing, he briefly referenced "that one thing that happened a while back…just want you to know it will never happen again, so you never have that on your mind." That was the only time in over three decades that it was ever mentioned.

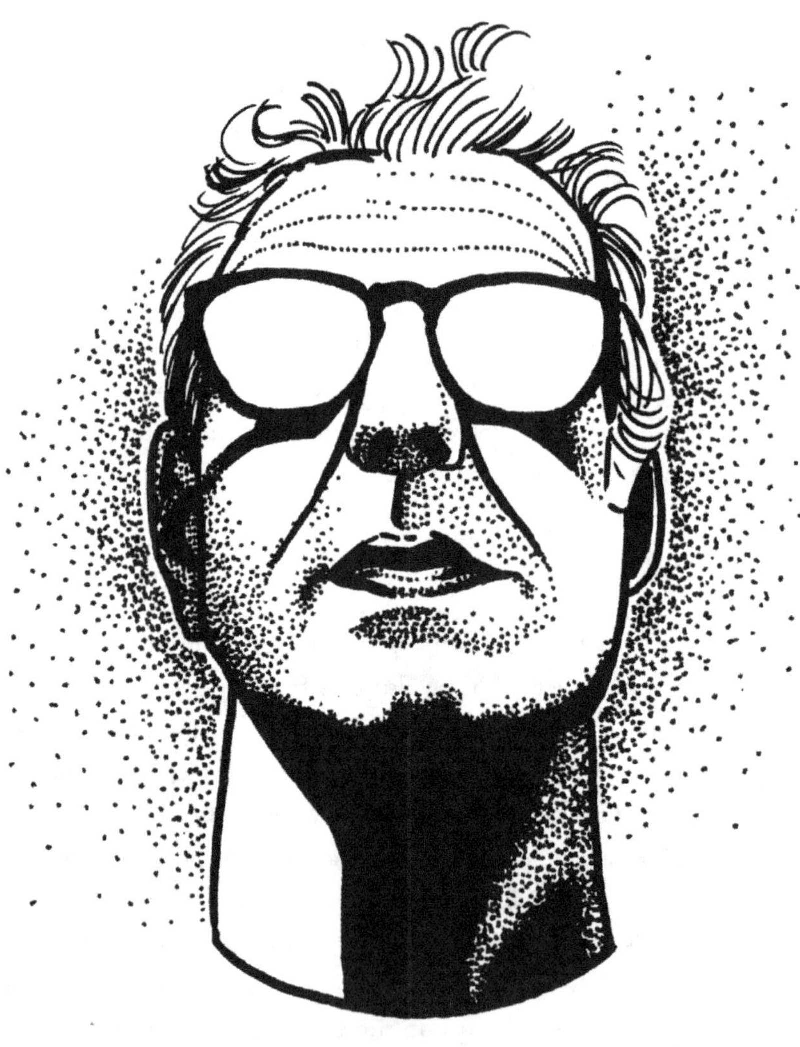

And then, on what would have been the perfect June day, his final act completed his story with devastating predictability.

Am I different from my father? Yes and no. Having symbolic references of him tattooed on my skin is a daily reminder that, in some very real ways, I am like him, of him. I'm not above anything. It would be like a recovering alcoholic bragging to other addicts about how easy it is not to drink. They're either a liar or were never an addict in the first place. The tattoos are also my reminder of what the "worst" outcome really means for those who remain and then must live with it every day. People who kill themselves suffer tremendously — beyond what most people can fathom. I believe that anytime someone kills themselves they are simultaneously killing a piece of those left behind. I also believe that, for most people, if they knew and understood that, it would impact their decision. But those final decisions are often made in fleeting moments where everything goes to shit at once in the brain. If only they could get through those critical few minutes, they might not make the same decision — and history is rewritten.

My father had his demons. We all do, whether we acknowledge them or try to stuff them away (which never works; they always come out). But he also had his better angels — his lighter, brighter side that was special…magical, in fact.

Despite being a short-fused, larger-than-life figure that was quick to throw a punch when justified, he was also a hugger. None of that bullshit high-five, see-ya-later shit. He would pull you in, hug the air out of you, and give you a kiss goodbye or hello. And not just an air peck fake BS kiss like some asshat in Beverly Hills. He'd smack a big one on the side of your neck. Not creepy, just enthusiastic. He was a big powerful dude, with powerful words and a powerful presence anywhere he went. Part of that meant pulling you in, holding you in, and showing — not telling — that he loved you.

And while I've worked hard to avoid and shed some of his parenting traits as a father, this is one of the ways I strive to emulate him. I make a point of hugging and kissing my kids frequently, especially when I know I may not be as present walking in the door as I want to be, depending on "life" at any given moment. So whenever I can, I stop, look at my kids — three Irish triplets simultaneously laughing / playing / crying / fighting and one 15-year-old glued to her iPad — and

I pull them in so damn close. They don't know now how much each embrace counts, but they will remember later…when it matters the most.

There are no redo's in parenting. You *will* fuck something up (a lot). But sometimes those mistakes — as painful and horrible as they might be — are the greatest gifts. My father's missteps continue to guide me in my own journey as a father, one fumbling day at a time. He is forever etched in my skin, a reminder of his eternal place in my heart. When I hug my kids, he is hugging them. Each embrace brings us closer, even in his absence.

◆ ◆ ◆

CI VEDIAMO PRESTO

THE ITALIAN BOOK Adam Greco, Nursery School Teacher

I currently have my feet, ankles, thigh, sleeves, entire chest, and back done. I'm slowly working on finishing my entire torso and then moving to my legs. I enjoy the duality of spending my free time immersed in tattoo subculture, and then spending my work week as a nursery schoolteacher.

The standards of ethics that I prioritize in my life I partially learned from my amazing father. Four years ago, my father lost his battle to cancer, quite literally before my eyes. That experience broke me down. The only thing I had left to remember him by were our memories and the few possessions he left behind. He always wanted my siblings and me to learn Italian, so he hand-wrote out an entire notebook full of Italian phrases for us. Two years after he passed, I finally worked up the courage to help my mom go through his belongings – and I found that purple and white marble notebook. One phrase in particular resonated with me: "ci vediamo presto" – "I'll see you soon."

Getting tattooed used to be something entirely different to me. It once meant self expression and enjoying the beauty of the art. Now it has become another way I can connect myself to my father and honor him. Today, with a beautiful daughter and a family of my own, the void of his presence is felt tenfold. Of all my tattoos, this very small tattoo holds the most meaning. It's a simple reminder that my time with him is not over, and one day I will be reunited with my hero.

KIDS

THE ULTIMATE CLEAN SLATE

It was 2007. A few days before we left for Ethiopia to pick up Zoe, the four-month-old baby we were adopting, we received a call from the agency warning us that she might not be alive when we arrived.

In Sub-Saharan Africa, thousands of infants die daily of dehydration and other preventable causes, and Zoe had been taken to a local hospital, unconscious and suffering from severe dehydration. Fifteen years ago, communication was very limited with Ethiopia (it still has its limits, even today), so we did not know when we would get an update or any other details. We just knew there was a very real possibility she would not make it. Needless to say, it was crippling news. And as hard as it is to be by your sick child's bedside in a hospital, facing unknowns and feeling helpless, the reality of not physically being with our sick baby in Ethiopia —was unbearable. Decisions about her care were out of our control at this point — we didn't even know what kind of medical facility she was in — so our imaginations ran wild, catastrophizing the situation.

I was at work when I got the news, and my mind raced in a million directions. I went down to the parking lot and just started…walking in circles.

With my head down to the pavement. I didn't look up — couldn't — because I didn't want to make eye contact. I couldn't face any small talk or friendly "How are you?" questions. I wanted zero human interaction. After thirty minutes of walking in circles, staring at the pavement, as hopeless and desperate as I have ever been, I closed my eyes tight and said something along the lines of, "Hey God, it's me…the guy who pretty much only checks in when he's fucked. Well, here I am again, but it's not just me this time. So please, *please* help our baby through this. She's been through enough already. Please. And thank you very much."

I didn't realize it, but I had stopped walking when I closed my eyes (which probably helped me avoid walking into a car or wall). When I opened my eyes, there was a beat-up old car I'd never seen before in our parking lot. The license plate staring me in the face read "NGDSHND." Anyone can make whatever they want of those seven letters. To me, instantly, it read as "In God's Hand." I ran back to my office to get a camera to snap a photo of the plate. But when I returned minutes later, the car was gone. Never saw it in our lot again.

The next day, we got an update that Zoe was recovering and had regained consciousness.

After that rocky start, the term "helicopter parent" would absolutely apply to how I operated. I joke that I was the reason that term was created. I was NEVER gonna let anything happen to my kid again. Ever. She'd already been through enough. So I fucking HOVERED.

It's possible I took it a *weeeee* bit too far with her. At eight years old, she didn't have much of a desire to ride a bike, perhaps because I ran along side of her like the secret service guards the Presidential limo. At one point, she'd had enough and screamed at me from the playground in front of her friends: *"DAD, YOU ARE SINGLE-HANDEDLY PREVENTING ME FROM CONQUERING MY FEARS IN LIFE!"* (Her exact words, I swear.) I keep my hands outreached to keep her from falling — always, anywhere. Does that make me a bad dad?

There is a tendency amongst first-time parents to lack balance. In addition to the hovering, I was obsessed with soaking in all the moments. Right before flying to Africa, I bought a new camera. I vowed to record every moment of Zoe's life. When she was around six or seven, I took my Mac to the Apple store for an upgrade. The "genius" asked if I was a professional photographer because…I had over 50,000 photos of her. It was my way of saving the moment the only way I knew how.

When Zoe was finally in our arms, it was pure ecstasy. Unlike biological parents, we weren't with her in utero or at her birth or even in those precious early months. So the anticipation — and anxiety — skyrocketed. The moment we got her back to America, I knew she was safe and secure in her happy crib, surrounded by people who loved her and would care for her. But instead of relaxing, my mind went into overdrive. Now I needed to protect her, provide security for her. Not a bad instinct, but perhaps one that needed…a bit more balance.

A few days after we returned home, I left for a grueling four-day shoot. I brought her picture with me and had it on my nightstand in the hotel room and would stare at it before bed and when I woke up in the morning. I felt guilt around my absence. I'd already missed so much. Now I was missing… more. I wasn't holding her, feeding her, hearing her little sounds. I wasn't out at bars or taking guys' trips; I was working. More than ever. And in my line of work, 9-5 at the office was rare. Creative development, filming, production, is a 24/7 mindset. To be good, to be successful at it, you can't just be passionate; you need to be a bit (a lot) obsessive. And I was.

Eight years later, we were ready for more kids.

Jaxon Wolf was born in Alabama. (Wolf was the nickname my father had given me as a child, so it became Jaxon's middle name — and of course, future tattoo material.) I was on my way to a meeting with Jennifer Lopez and her manager when I got the call that Jaxon's birth mother was in labor, so I bailed on the meeting, scrambled to the airport, flew to New Orleans, and drove to Alabama.

I arrived at the hospital very late at night, and there was nowhere for me to sleep. So they let me peek in on my boy from the window without waking up all the babies, and then they put me in a tiny office (barely bigger than a closet), and I sort of slept on a big chair until the babies "woke up" the next morning. What I did not know was that the space I was crashing in was actually the "lactation teaching room." Needless to say, the next morning, I was not what the beaming new moms were expecting when I opened the door…

Later that day, I sat in the nursery with Jaxon. He was a fresh start for me. Like Bruce said at the end of "Long Time Comin'," *"And I ain't gonna fuck it up this time."* I did not want history to repeat itself with this father/son relationship. The sins of my father, as well as my own, would not be repeated in my relationship with my son, Jaxon.

When Jaxon was born, Zoe was already almost nine years old and was already drifting out of the phase of always wanting to be with Mom and Dad. I wanted back those early years to hold her again and just rest my attention on nothing but her.

Living in the moment is not a natural thing for me. My second tattoo ever was a Japanese kanji symbol that means "live for today" / "live for the moment." I didn't get the tattoo to preach to others or share any wisdom I had on this subject. I knew my entire life I struggled in this area, and this was my first "reminder-to-self" tattoo. My way of forever saying "DO THIS!" every time I looked in the mirror. Your mind can race about all sorts of good, positive things, but if it's perpetually spinning, you are never fully present. Being fully present is what I didn't do enough of with Zoe when she was little, and what I've made a concerted effort to do more of with my younger kids now. And even though Zoe's now a teenage and I compete with iPads, phones, and her friends for attention — I try to soak up every precious moment with her that much more. I will always believe that your first child is when you truly understand the meaning of the word "love" for the first time. Becoming a parent awakened feelings in me I could not have imagined existed.

After Jaxon's birth, I remember two things so vividly: 1) The head nurse with a powerful Alabama accent asked me about scheduling his circumcision, to which I replied, "NO. You would not spray paint over Michelangelo's Sistine Chapel! You are not touching my boy!" and 2) I insisted that the nurse write in his medical chart, "Incredible looking boy." She (naturally) resisted, but when I wouldn't let up, she finally relented. When she asked me why, I said, "So now I can say it's a medically documented fact."

Jaxon had serious medical issues from birth, and we had a night nurse at times because he couldn't sleep for more than an hour or so at a time. One morning, the nurse came upstairs while we were having coffee and told us she had a vision overnight, in which she saw his baby sisters at the edge of the bed next to him. We laughed and dismissed it. (Jaxon's birth mom would not have been able to have more kids even if she wanted to…or so we thought.)

A few weeks later, we were on a family vacation in Maui, where they have tourist shops where you can "buy a shell and get a free pearl inside." Zoe really wanted to do it, so we finally said ok. The gig is the locals sell you the shell, then have you make a wish before you open it. She opened her shell, but it had TWO pearls, not one. We asked Zoe what she wished for: "Twin baby sisters." We laughed. "Yeah, that ain't happening."

The following week, we heard from Jaxon's birth mom for the first time since we parted ways at the hospital after his birth. She reached out to say she was pregnant again. She didn't have a due date, nor did she know the sex, but she said she was the biggest she'd ever been. We discussed what it meant for us if we adopted another baby, especially so soon after Jaxon, plus all the medical factors we were already dealing with. As we tried to wrap our heads around the prospect of a third child, we mentioned this to our nurse in passing. "Ah yes, the twins are coming," she replied matter-of-factly. Once again, we laughed. "Ah no — not twins. Just one baby. And she doesn't know the sex yet." The nurse replied, without skipping a beat, "It is twins. Girls. They visit me and Jaxon each night. They will be magical just like Jaxon and Zoe."

The birth mom went silent for about a week. No calls, no texts — totally unreachable. Finally, we heard from her: Twins. Girls.

(One of my tattoos of the twins includes a special pair of pearls. Wishes do come true.)

Harper and Ayana are my twin miracles. My double jackpot. I remember the doctor saying, "We need to take Harper out prematurely because of the gastroschisis, but we also need to leave them in utero as long as possible to benefit Ayana, who could otherwise make it to full term." I was so struck by that reality. Not only twins, but the weight of a medical procedure that was beneficial for one and could work against the other. Wanna feel out of control? That hits the mark.

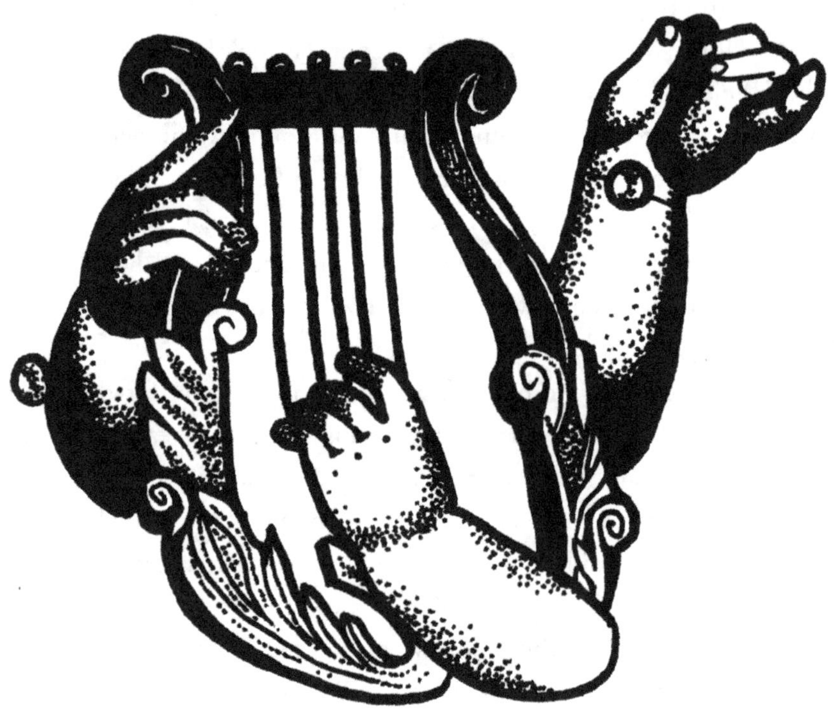

Gastroschisis is a birth defect where the baby's intestines form outside of their body. Harper was barely over four pounds at birth — yet still was considered "the big kid" in the NICU, where some babies weigh as little as a pound. My eyes still fill with tears just writing those words. It's a club only other parents who are in it can relate to, and certainly not one you ever hope to join, but once you are in, you become a hardcore motherfucker committed to whatever it takes to help your baby — no matter what. When the NICU nurses (aka heroes) would let me hold Harper, it took so much time for them just to spread out all the life-saving medical tubes and cables attached to her so they could scoop her out of her medical crib and place her in my arms. My God she was tiny. I would sit there for hours, wondering how this tiny lil' shell could hold a heart, lungs, and all that kept her alive.

One of the most painfully hard but necessary things all parents learn — one way or another — is you are so fucking NOT in control. *Especially* when it comes to your kids. With Zoe, I was convinced I could control (and therefore fix) any problem, issue, pain — whatever it was. By the time Harper and Ayana were born, I had been thoroughly checked on those arrogant and naive instincts: these four babies completely upended, kicked in my teeth, and forced me to learn that when it comes to your own kids, you sign up for a lifetime of feeling out of control. So even though Harper was born with major medical challenges, I was in a better mindset to approach it and get through it. (As opposed to flying home from Ethiopia with Zoe, where if she had sneezed, I probably would have taken over the plane and made an emergency landing at the nearest hospital.)

After three months of uncertainty in the Alabama NICU, she was finally well enough to come home. The doctors wanted her on breast milk because it helps with tummy wounds, so I joined a local breastfeeding Facebook group. I didn't realize I was the only dude member. It was made up of lactating women who would bottle and donate their extra breast milk to babies whose moms could not "feed." Obviously, breastfeeding was not a viable option for us, but we wanted the best for Harps. So when one of the FB ladies said she had extra milk ready and to just show up the next morning with a jug, I did. She opened the door and saw…ME. Pajamas (it was early morning), tank top (it was summer and warm, tattoo sleeves fully bared), cigar in mouth (was a nice morning for a Dominican robusto smoke), with a big, empty jug in my hand. She *SCREEEAMED* for her husband. I guess I wasn't quite what she expected.

I believe my kids' hardships — how they were born into the world, their separation from a birth mother, their medical issues — while challenging, also created resilience. They have an inner strength, determination, and survival instinct that gives them an edge.

Watching their resilience-in-action has helped shape my own adult life considerably. So many people (both young and old) make excuses and point fingers for anything and everything. When I observe my kids overcoming obstacles, they are always looking forward, full steam ahead. It enables me to look at my daily life, and the issues and frustrations that arise, and I remind myself that nothing in front of me, no obstacle or setback, even comes close to what my kids have already been through, even at their young ages. So if they don't point fingers and make excuses, how can I? They have empowered me not to blame anyone for my errors or wounds. I have four remarkable reminders every waking moment of the day that life is worth living.

I've never been anything but proud and grateful for being blessed with each of my kids. The chances of winning the lottery are in the billions, but I hit the jackpot four separate times.

Growing up, I never thought much about being a father one way or the other. I was more focused on figuring out the relationship with my own father than thinking about becoming one myself.

Whenever I heard people talk about their desire to have kids of their own and said they wanted a kid "with my eyes", or "who looks like Suzie", or "I hope my kid gets this from wife" — it was always a big disconnect for me. I felt...out of place. 'Cause I never felt the desire to pass on "me" genetically. It just never meant a damn thing to me. I always felt people had a bizarre fascination with their "bloodline" and "transferring their lineage." Some of the world's greatest leaders, athletes, and genius thinkers had biological kids that were...confirmed shitheads. It just never meant two fucks to me — any of it.

That's probably why adoption was so natural for me. In many ways, it was a clean slate: no baggage or second guessing. If my kid did something stupid, I couldn't blame it on my own shitty genes. I was just a shitty parent then. When I adopted my kids, I never perceived them as different for being adopted any more than I would if they were my biological offspring. I KNOW there is no possible way any human loves their kids more than I love mine. It's just something you know in your soul on the deepest level. It's like loving someone exponentially more than breathing air. I think if my kids were my biological children, I would perhaps see some of my own flaws and personal failings in them. But instead, I see four blank slates, and as Bruce sings, a chance to "not fuck it up this time."

Before the world fell under the spell of Facebook, people kept blogs. Today, blogs tend to be tied to a business or a brand. But fifteen years ago, personal blogs were the long-format way for people to share their life events and journeys. One day, my kids' mom and I read a blog about a family that had recently adopted from Ethiopia. It was sweet, special, and genuine. They looked like a happy family. At that same time, we were trying to have kids "the old fashioned, biological way." We waited a while after getting married to try and start a family, and by then, we were both inching closer to 40 than we were to 30. We were just about to start exploring some of the fertility options (which we were not overly excited about) when we found this adoption blog. I don't have anything against fertility treatments — I think they are generally wonderful opportunities to help people create the families that are right for them. It just didn't feel like the right approach for us. For starters, I already had reservations about walking into some sterile doctor's office, being handed a stack of magazines, and asked to "perform." I was extremely open to an alternative.

Soon, the adoption idea quickly went from looking at a blog to looking up adoption agencies, and within a matter of only a few days, we felt like we had landed 100 percent on our family plan. It seemed so wildly spontaneous, and yet, calmingly, absolutely right.

I'm not a fan of over-publicized adoptions. I call them "Facebook adoptions," where people make big announcements that can over-dramatize in a way that is made to seem more like a rescue than an adoption, so that the world will proclaim "how wonderful you guys are for adopting a child." I have seen this martyrdom escalate when it's a white family adopting a black child. I understand baby announcements. I get it. We did them; it's part of the joy of starting a family. But some adoptive parents have a Santa Claus complex, particularly if they are white and their baby is black. They pat themselves on the back for "rescuing kids." Adopting a baby is not "rescuing" a child from a burning building. Get the fuck over yourself. Some people give birth and get a baby that way. Others fill out a shit ton of paperwork for a year and get a baby that way. One way is no more heroic or special or "kind-hearted" than the other.

A friend of mine once introduced me and my daughter to his other friends and he referred to me as "my buddy Drew and his adopted daughter, Zoe." He had zero ill intentions and was actually just trying to connect his friends together, but regardless, I replied, "Nice to meet you guys, and how do you know my friend Steve here and his *biological* son, Michael?" Everyone froze. And he started apologizing. I told my buddy there was no apology needed, but I wanted him to see how fucking stupid it is to see things that way. As flawed humans, we always look for what makes us the slightest bit different versus the many things that make us all similar.

We get a lot of questions about why we chose Ethiopia, and of course, questions about race.

Navigating the adoption world has many variables, some known, but many unknown. There are facts, rumors, stories, misperceptions — and when you add all of that to being prospective new parents and the jumble of emotions tied to that, there's a LOT to consider. For us, international adoption presented a lot of benefits at that time. There were a few specific countries that were moving fairly quickly in terms of matching new babies and American families. Ethiopia was one of them. There were also certain "unknowns" for us about domestic adoption back then. *Would a birth parent show up on our doorstep six months after the adoption wanting to take our baby back?* While there are generally procedures and protections (for birth parents, children, and adoptive parents), there is no such thing as a perfect system, and certainly the world of adoptions, like any other, has its flaws and cracks in the system that, sadly, can be exploited by bad dudes.

The international option also provided — for me, at least — what felt like more of that "clean slate" I was searching for. And since Ethiopia was far, far away, it truly felt like a symbolic break from my past, all the mess and ugliness I saw in my own history. Her birth felt like a true rebirth: The birth of a new baby, devoid of sin, pure light without a shred of darkness. It was a rebirth for me, not only as a parent but as a grown man, the opportunity to build and create the family I wanted.

I was also mesmerized by Ethiopia. Known as the "birthplace of civilization," where the oldest human remains on record were found (aka "Lucy"), Ethiopia is also believed to hold the lost Ark of the Covenant, according to legend. Ethiopians are a strong, majestic, ass-kicking group of motherfuckers who have never been conquered in their entire history — other than a brief window from 1935-1941, when Italy invaded and colonized. But they got their asses handed back to them pretty quickly, and the upside is, even today, you can have some of the best Italian food in the world…in Ethiopia. (True fact: Wolfgang Puck, who married an Ethiopian woman, has stated the best Italian food he had was in Ethiopia.) And here's the kicker: FUCKING COFFEE, DUDE. Damn straight. E-T-H-I-O-P-I-A, coffee's birthplace. That alone made this East African kingdom the capital of the world in my mind.

When adopting Zoe, the fact that she was a different race than us didn't have the impact people assume it would have on our process. We wanted a baby to help build a family. We were not trying to make a statement. I grew up being one of the only Jewish kids in my entire school and neighborhood. There was only one black family in our neighborhood, and that kid happened to be my age. We became close friends — pretty much best friends, from a young age. I don't think we were old enough or attuned enough to understand that both of us "not belonging" helped bring us closer together, but I imagine there was something to that subconsciously.

I knew what it felt like not to be welcome. It was New Jersey, and back then there was a lot of ignorance. I believe there is a difference between ignorance and hatred. It's not always easy to spot the difference, but there is one. One year, during Halloween, some kids dressed up as Klansmen and came trick-or-treating at our door. Another time someone painted a Nazi swastika on our driveway. Kids tend to tease and call each other names, so more than a few times, I was called "Drew the Jew." If anything, those things made me feel closer and more connected to others who were not part of "the majority." As I got older and became more comfortable taking care of myself and any problems that came along, I took comfort in being on the side of the minority or anyone being picked up or taken advantage of by a stronger power. It's just where I saw myself belonging, fitting it.

So adopting a black child did not give me any pause or hesitation whatsoever. But that doesn't mean it didn't affect them. When Zoe was six or seven, she came home from school one day and asked me if we were a "biracial family." It was honest-to-God the first time I ever realized that from a terminology perspective, I guess we were. But then I told her I never thought about color, and all I knew and cared about was that she was my daughter and I was her Dad. I guess my mind was simplistic beyond what someone might expect on such a topic.

Years later, as racial tensions began flaring up, I did realize I needed to be more deliberately cognizant of how race could impact my kids, especially my son. In my head, my kids never had anything to worry about regarding race — or anything, really — 'cause I would be there to protect and handle and shield them, no matter the scope. But I (now) realize that is fucking naive. Whether it's race issues, a school shooter, a car accident…I'm not in all places at all times. So while I can jump in front of a car for them, and would, I may not always be there when the car is coming. And that's a life lesson that is hard to come to terms with as a parent. What if I am not there when one of them ever needs me?

Zoe was an only child until she was eight years old, and then very quickly had three baby siblings. That's when she became MUCH more interested in tattoos, because up until then, she got all the real estate on my body when it came to tattoos dedicated to my kids. Once I started adding my three lil's to the tattoos, Zoe kept count (and was very happily aware that she had more ink than her siblings).

I integrated my kids into my tattoos for several reasons: First, words fall short of describing the immeasurable role they play in my life. So it would be impossible to have tattoos tell my story without tying in my main cast. Second, even though I never thought of myself as an *adoptive* parent, and I never thought of my kids as "adopted" versus "biological," I did have this internal desire to prove to them — beyond any doubt — that we are FOREVER a family, with me as their dad. I didn't explain this reasoning for the tattoos to them, but kids are smart. When they see a tattoo with their name on it, and know it ain't washing off in the shower, it makes a point.

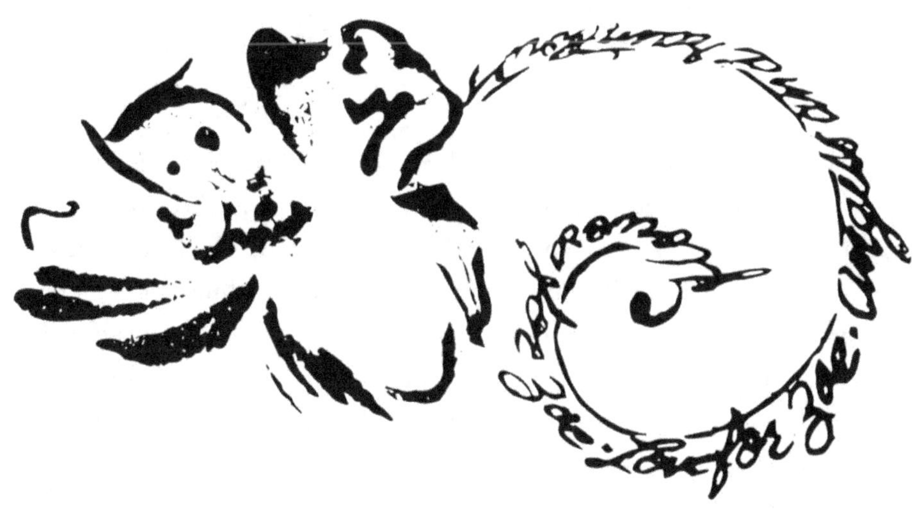

I've also tried to connect aspects of their identity with the tattoos. One of my first tattoos related to my kids was a flower design with some of the lyrics from "Flowers for Zoe," a song Lenny Kravitz wrote for his own daughter, Zoe. I thought it was beautiful: *"Flowers for Zoe / Love is for Zoe / Angels and rainbows / All kinds of things you can call your own."* So that became one of my special Zoe tattoos.

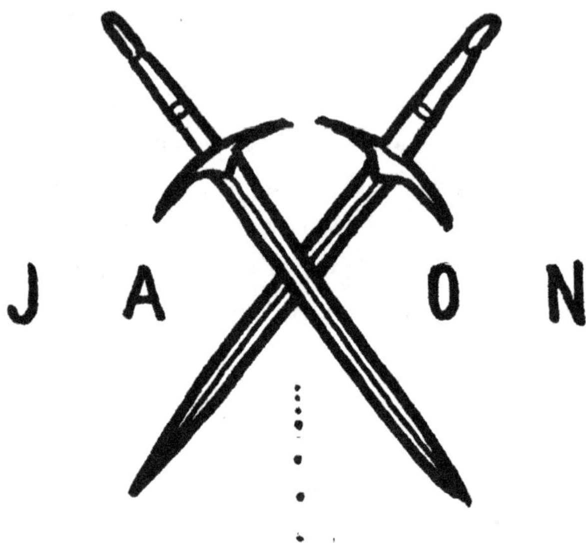

Jaxon faced medical issues since birth and is a true warrior. One of the most gut-wrenching experiences was watching him live with a tracheostomy tube in his neck for a period of time to help him breathe safely. Thankfully the trach was able to come out eventually, but it left a physical scar on him (and emotional scars on all of us). I didn't want him to look at his scar and see trauma or pain. I wanted him to see the incredibly brave, rock hard lil' dude he is. So on my own trach, in the same exact area, to match his scar, I had his name tattooed: JAXON. But instead of a normal letter X, we used two swords crossing. It's symbolic of a fighter who never quits, just like my boy.

The twins are just absolute characters and 24/7 Energizer bunnies, so they tend to trace the letters of their names with their fingers and are just now getting old enough to be more aware of the permanence and meaning.

I've thought about what kind of example I set for my kids with my tattoos. My main priority is that they are happy, so if getting tattoos brings them genuine happiness, I won't discourage it. Do I worry or freak the fuck out when I watch all four of them use markers and draw tattoos on their bodies? Yeah, kinda. But I worry less about the general concept of them getting tattoos and more about them not being thoughtful enough in their approach. It's easy at a young age to get excited about something one day and not so much the next. But if you get two full arm sleeves of tattoos when you're eighteen, are you really at a point where you know what you want on your arms for the rest of your life? Have you lived enough yet to know? I helped my niece get her first tattoo when she was sixteen because I wanted to ensure she got nice, safe, professional work done, since she was going to get a tattoo anyway, but I also did it because it was small and thoughtful (a memorial to her dad). Had she wanted "IRON MAIDEN" inked across her chest, Uncle Drew probably would have said, *No fucking way, kid.*

My boy told me the other day he wants a tattoo when he turns seven. (I haven't broken that news to his mom yet, 'cause she probably will break part of me when I do…). And as my daughter inches closer to dating age, I may find her bringing home guys with tattoos. I intend to be apprehensive of ANYONE my lil' girls ever date (even when they are 50 years old). But someone with tattoos can be a self-made billionaire, a Nobel Prize winner, a world leader, or just an all-around good human. And let's face it — there are serial killers and cannibals who have zero tattoos. So to judge a book by its cover in today's world is pretty moronic.

It's a weird irony, wanting to keep your kids safe and protect them from harm, while also wanting to set them up to live limitlessly, without a fear of failure. Three of my four kids have faced life-threatening medical issues. I know some families have it much worse, and I'm always thankful for how things have generally turned out (despite some ongoing medical issues). It fucks with you as a parent to see your kids be in medical situations you can't control or fix on your own. It's a pretty helpless, borderline unbearable process to endure.

I never feel like I picked my kids. I always believe they picked me. And I often thank them for picking me, for choosing me to be their dad, forever. A lot of people say to them, "Oh you're so lucky to be adopted by a nice family, to live by the beach…" I shut that down so fucking quick. It's the most ignorant comment a person could make. Why are my kids lucky? Because they have parents who love them, a home, food, and go to school? Do most non-adopted kids in America get told by strangers they are lucky for having parents? It's absurd. My kids didn't get a gift. *WE* got the gift of being their parents.

I remember Jaxon's birth mom telling us that she was deciding between us and one other adoptive family. She held up the "adoption books" of both families near her belly when Jaxon was in her womb and she whispered to her tummy, *Which family do you want to be with?* She said right then she felt a kick towards our book which was opened to a picture of me. And so that was the decision. He picked us. He picked me. (I later joked that maybe he was kicking me away, screaming in her tummy, *ANYONE BUT THIS BIG IDIOT WITH ALL THE TATTOOS!*) But the truth is, my boy picked us. And I know my three girls did, too. No matter what the world throws at me, I've already won — four times over.

Both of my parents whisper in my ear as I parent. Our parents, regardless of how close (or not) we are to them, play a role in shaping the kind of parent we will be. My father is no exception. He taught me the things I don't want to repeat, as well as the lessons I very much want to pass on: the giant hugs, the feeling of knowing you had Rocky Balboa in your corner for life. And the value of loyalty.

There is a saying: *The road to hell is paved with good intentions.* I think it's a stupid fucking saying. I've learned that someone's intentions, their heart, what they hoped, wanted, and wished for someone, especially their kids…it means something. It means a lot. People fail. Parents probably fail the most of any creatures on earth. In ways big or small, we are all victims of our parents' failings. And we also benefit from them: those failings are our guide. Good, bad, and usually both, that's the only map we are given.

Like all parents, I want my kids to be happy, healthy, and financially secure. But I also equally hope that their lives have no limits — no boundaries, no preconceived expectations about what is typical and expected of them. I want my kids to write their own stories and live their own adventures: not on paper, but by living, doing, seeking, finding, getting lost as fuck and then joyfully finding themselves (as well as some amazing travel companions along their journey).

So, these days, when I hear my parents' voices in my head, they whisper their best intentions. My father's uniquely salty, attention-grabbing voice calmly tells me what he wanted, wished, and hoped for me. I respond, assuring him he provided me with everything I needed and more. And that I hope I've done a few things along the way to make him proud.

Each time my kids were placed in my arms for the very first time, I whispered in each of their ears, while nobody else was around: "Thank you for picking me to be your daddy. I love you more than you will ever know or words can say. I wish for you a magical life." Four times. Nothing has changed for me since those days. Same wish, same magical kids.

BUY THE TICKET, TAKE THE RIDE

MY ACCIDENTAL RETURN TO STORYTELLING VIA A PANDEMIC, A PODCAST, AND A POP LEGEND

When I left Reno, I was busted. Literally. Broke, failed at my career plan, and physically in shreds. My chronic neck pain, which flared up around the time my career took a nosedive, was unbearable, and I was popping muscle relaxers like Tic Tacs (and not for fun). My hair was also falling out from all the stress, pain, and anxiety. It was rock bottom for me.

Twenty-four years later, my life was unrecognizable. I had four spectacular kids and built a successful L.A. agency working with mega-brands, A-list celebrities, and professional athletes, plus I was spending invaluable time with business icons who were already at the place I was focused on reaching.

Despite those obvious successes, there was one itch left unscratched: I hadn't found a way to fill that void of storytelling. I thought that part of the dream died when I limped out of Reno in my U-Haul. Turns out, it just took a detour.

When Covid hit and the world shut down, we were fucked. Man, I used to say that while some people had contingency plans for A-E, I had contingency plans for A-Z, and then AA-ZZ. There was no scenario in my business life I was not prepared for or had not anticipated as a potential reality. Some people like to zone out and forget about work, but planning for contingencies is how I relax. I love building and creating, so it's comforting for me to think about ways to protect what I love. That may sound like a contradiction to my "No Plan B" mantra that's tattooed across my finger (and ingrained in my brain and soul), but in reality, planning for contingencies is one of the things that always gives me an edge, so I don't have to worry about a Plan B in life.

Anyway… Some agencies have a good backup system for client files and data. Others are more reckless. Me? I have the cloud, PLUS a triple-tiered backup system that includes internal fireproof safes able to withstand intense flames for more than thirty minutes and protect against floods or water leaks, PLUS another copy that is locked and secured in nearly indestructible off-site safes.

I used to joke somewhat seriously that I was ready for the apocalypse.

And then — we got hit by an apocalypse. A *real* one, in the form of a global pandemic. Overnight, the world came crashing down, and with it, many clients who owed us significant money froze their own spending on a dime. Even some companies with a shit ton of capital reserves simply decided to join the "freeze all payments" movement, including the money they owed me. This included money we FRONTED on their behalf. We're talking seven-figures — *FROZEN*. Might as well have been gone forever, 'cause that money no longer existed for us when we needed it most. Simultaneously, every single production we had underway stopped. Overnight. No more billings or fees generating. Nothing. Talk about a full DFS. Dead Fucking Stop.

I still had a whole team of editors, designers, animators, writers, support staff, creative directors, web people…but what the fuck do they work on if there is nothing being filmed or produced? Ya can't edit thin air. Besides, L.A. county was locked down and everyone was required by the state to work from home. But all of our edit bays, data systems, storage, hard drives were wired into our physical office — not spread out over 27 homes.

So I spoke to the team and reminded them of two things:

1) *Every crisis creates new opportunity.* It wasn't an original phrase, but I 1,000% believe it. I told everyone this would be the start of something bigger and better than any of us could imagine at that moment. (Pretty sure people wanted to drug test me considering the world was literally closing and showed no signs of getting "back to normal.")

2) *We would survive…to THRIVE.* Again, it seemed crazy, a total denial of reality, but I didn't want people having the mentality of treading water. It was obvious whatever this "Covid" thing was, we were in for the long haul (and a helluva a lot longer than I'd imagined back then), and I wanted everyone to focus not on "getting by," but on what our eventual success and reinvention would look like. I wanted to give our team permission to get excited about the possibilities versus living in fear.

My attorney and financial advisors, on the other hand, very understandably wanted me to consider the idea of closing up shop to secure whatever remaining assets we had left in the bank. And then we'd maybe have something small left to start over whenever the storm let up. Production companies and agencies like mine were folding like chairs overnight. I trusted and respected my advisors — "my adults" — because they were genuinely looking out for me and my long-term best interest in the midst of only unknowns. Every day I was hemorrhaging whatever money we had left. It was hard to say no to them.

But among all the unknowns at that moment, one of the things I did know is that I only move in one direction: forward. I knew if I went backwards — not a side step or slowing down to let a storm pass…but fucking backwards…close up shop…cash in your last $20 chips and admit to yourself (and the world) that you just got your ass handed to you — I knew personally it would be a direction I would not return from.

The instinct to tread water makes sense. If you are lost at sea and you don't tread water, ya drown. But what actually enables you to keep treading water, through the freezing temps, the exhaustion, the mental fatigue, the self-doubt, the fear…is purpose and hope. *What will you do WHEN you survive?* You maintain belief that someone — anyone — is coming to rescue you. That is what keeps people treading water in dire situations. People have done it for upwards of 30 hours and survived. But if someone KNEW for certain (or was convinced in their own mind) that it was hopeless, I suspect they would stop treading and drown in an hour — or far sooner.

I needed hope, too. And purpose. For *me.*

As I watched 27 people say goodbye and walk out of the office, all at the same time, I stared into space in total silence for a few hours. Then, over the initial sting and fog of the shock, moved into the reimagining phase: I walked around the middle of our agency floor, staring at the empty rows of desks that filled the big open area, as my eyes scanned the desolate shell of our 8,000 square foot empty nothingness. The list of things I didn't have at that moment was longer than those kickass CVS receipts. And the list of what we *did* have? It could fit on a Post-it note: A few cameras, some audio gear, an empty office space I could do whatever I wanted with (especially since I was in a lease I had to keep paying whether I showed up or slept all day).

Then, as I stared blankly at the empty space, I tried to think of ways to use what we did have versus the endless list of what we didn't have. I remembered that before Covid hit, we had begun researching the idea of advertising on podcasts for some of our client brands, and the research was impressive. But that was advertising on someone else's *successful, existing* podcast. Starting our own actual podcast? Sure. Why the fuck not?

So I ripped out all of the desks and custom-sized workspace furniture we had paid a fortune for, texted a friend who designed large production sets for me over the years to see if he could build us a small production set in the middle of our office, and then banged out a list of every interesting person I knew who could be a potential guest.

All I needed was a name. What do you call a podcast with no rules or bosses or outside accountability? And no sponsors or advertisers to answer to or ask for permission …for anything. A podcast with stories nobody would see *anywhere* but here? As *Not* Seen On TV?

Yep, that works.

And BOOM. We had a podcast.

Soon after we launched, the Britney Spears conservatorship story was a major media topic. I had not been following it and was not overly familiar with the details around it, but apparently her brother, Bryan Spears, was willing to do an interview with us. I thought it would be an epic waste of time — so much so that I only agreed to it for five to ten minutes. I planned to cut it off and not post it on our YouTube page if it turned out as pointless as I assumed it would be.

Preparing for the podcast, I read up on the #FreeBritney Movement. To my surprise, it was extremely compelling. This wasn't a handful of aging, die-hard Britney groupies hoping for an autograph. This was an organized, functional, hyper-passionate, *sizable* force who seemed like they were genuinely battling to right a wrong and provide protection for someone who was vulnerable. This was much (much) larger than a pop star in a dysfunctional family. So instead of five minutes, I spoke with Britney's brother Bryan for well over an hour. And I asked certain questions that, it turns out, millions of people wanted answers to.

When we posted the podcast on YouTube and clips on Instagram, I figured maybe twenty people would watch. But the next morning, I got calls and emails from media outlets around the world. We were all over the place…countless news channels, along with every digital publication imaginable. I was getting texts from people I hadn't been in touch with since high school, people who had seen or heard about our interview with Bryan Spears. I was asked to appear in numerous documentaries, all racing to tell their version of the Britney Spears story — but I turned them all down, including the paid gigs. Why? Because she was a woman clearly in distress and quite possibly being held against her will all these years. I didn't want to feed the media frenzy by providing content I would not retain editorial control over. (Plus, it was the same media that had for years harassed a youthful Britney Spears, labeled her as "crazy" and cruelly mocked her relentlessly without mercy). I felt our podcast interview showed a very fair, balanced, and clear depiction of her brother Bryan, in his own words. I wanted our interview to stand on its own and allow people to make their own assessments. So, as far as I was concerned, my part was done. I wasn't looking to cash in on someone else's pain and hurt.

The documentary, *Framing Britney Spears*, produced by *The New York Times*, which became a huge Emmy-nominated hit and, some say, played a significant role in exposing and ending the conservatorship — and, yes, I also turned them down for an interview, *but* they took my podcast interview and used it in their movie anyway. Fuckers. When that film came out, strangers stopped me on the street: *"It's the guy from the Britney Spears movie!"* (That's actually how I found out I was in it — from strangers on the street telling me.)

When I agreed to do the interview with Bryan, I knew Britney Spears was a singer, but I couldn't even name three of her songs. (Truthfully, I couldn't name two. I knew there was one that went "Oops, I did it again," but other than that...) Needless to say, I had no idea what was happening in her life. I didn't understand the Britney world, wasn't aware there was a "Free Britney" movement, didn't know jack or shit about Britney Spears. So the day of the interview, despite my best efforts to prep with little time, I made what amounts to a few...teeny weeny... not-so-small mistakes: I asked about her daughters (she has boys) — not once, but a few times. I fucked up the pronunciation of "conservatorship" like seven times (or more). It got to the point that I would stumble on the word so badly and so often that Bryan would say the word for me. (In fairness, it's a tricky word to pronounce! Say it out loud now — *see what I mean?*) As a result of these fuck-ups, people thought my "acting" was hilarious and great. Comments noted, "That journalist was brilliant, he kept playing dumb about Britney to get her brother to let his guard down." That wasn't entirely true: While I have been known to intentionally "lower the bar" for beneficial reasons, this happened to be a case where I simply was not well-versed in the history of Britney, nor was I expecting to be interviewing her brother in what was already becoming one of the largest celebrity PR/media firestorms in years.

(On another podcast episode, my guest was a celebrity rehab sobriety coach. I asked him how one of his more famous clients was doing. Me: "So, Bob…how is the Mayor doing these days? Is he still sober? Has he stayed on track, or has he slipped?" Bob: "He's dead. He died of cancer years ago, Drew." Me: "I shall consider myself updated, Bob. Good to know." But the reality is, I try to balance preparation with keeping it unrehearsed and in the moment, even when it means an occasional "oops, I did it again.")

I thought I left all my storytelling and journalism dreams behind in Reno decades prior. After that, the game changed. I shifted focus. It became about practical survival, not what-you-want-to-be-when-you-grow-up fantasies. So when I launched *As Not Seen On TV* to feed my soul and occupy my staff (instead of laying them off) during the pandemic, I envisioned it as a side project to tell some meaningful stories and kill time before work-as-usual could resume. It felt like the healthiest outlet for me to channel my energy and frustration. Plus, I still had that itch.

So there I was, making headlines and fielding interview requests (and turning them all down) from the media outlets I'd longed to work for so many years ago. The universe has an ironic — and at times, twisted — sense of humor.

On a side note, it turns out Britney did end up watching our podcast interview we did with her brother once she was free from the conservatorship. In a social media exchange that was shared by media outlets around the world, she referred to me as "kind" and cited a specific example of how I handled the interview. I've been called lots of less-than-favorable things in my life, so "kind" might be close to my #1 favorite.

Post-Reno, telemarketing helped me tread water while I carved my niche in the infomercial world, the success of which allowed me to launch my agency, employ a special collection of people, and provide for my family. It certainly wasn't what

I'd envisioned, but I considered it a win. Then Covid took a wrecking ball to that success and stability, despite my extensive contingency plans. But in the rubble, I found a new medium, a new audience, a new outlet that reawakened a part of me that had been dormant for too long. I interviewed Navy SEALs, entrepreneurs, renowned doctors, a "philosophical" retired mafia hitman, and everyday heroes whose stories I wanted to amplify. *As Not Seen On TV* is not currently making me millions. But that's not the point. It's storytelling — *on my terms* — which is priceless to me.

I've owned my own business or worked for myself most of my adult life. I can't imagine it any other way. But the reality is, running a business and being the boss doesn't always make you feel like the boss. In my agency world, producing for worldwide brands over the years, the clients were always the real bosses. They wrote the checks. So you had the CEO of the brand calling the shots, along with whatever internal staff they assigned to manage a project. There were times we had fifteen clients at the same time — all "mini bosses" to interact with daily. Plus, at our peak, we had an internal staff of around 35 people. That's a lot of personalities, all with opinions, needs, wants, and issues. By the time a project is complete, it's hard to remember YOU are the actual boss and not just some dude with a lot of salaries and rent to pay, a shit ton of liability, and way too many egos and personalities to manage.

With *As Not Seen On TV*, there was none of that. No bosses, no rules, no outside noise. Whatever I wanted to do, say, show, I had 100% creative FREEDOM. *Finally.*

As Not Seen On TV gave me the freedom to be…ME. People knew what I looked like and some thought they "knew" me. But few — if any — did. Some people expressed their disdain for the profanity I would occasionally (often) use on our podcast. Or complained about the t-shirt I wore on-set a few times that said *"Fuck the rules."* But despite those protests, I talked about what I wanted, when, how, and with whomever-the-fuck I wanted. Even if nobody watched, I loved finding and telling these stories. They needed to be told. Sometimes it takes removing the monetary factor to unlock the most compelling storytelling: *As Not Seen On TV* gave me the idea to eventually launch my tattoo-inspired series, "Think. Ink. Drink." That was the gold I found in the big pile of pandemic garbage: I rediscovered my voice. I completely detached from the financial outcome or even the audience reception. Whether we were broadcasting to an audience of one or one million, I got to be me. And I was finally comfortable in that skin.

My best friend died way too young. I still see his face and speak with him every day; his voice and unique personal language echoes in my head. He also continues to occasionally inspire some of my new tattoos.

During summers in our teens, Terry and I screwed around at the Jersey Shore. We lifeguarded during the days, and at night, I bartended and Terry waited tables. One summer, he loaned me a book: Hunter S. Thompson's *Fear and Loathing in Las Vegas*. I don't know if any single book can change a person's life, but that book, that summer, changed the way I thought about life and what it meant not just to live life, but to experience it.

One of the things that made me value my friendship with Terry was his ability to do this one specific thing I wanted so badly, but which I lacked the "skill" or innate ability to do: He lived in the moment. Like nobody I ever met before (or would again, to this day). He didn't need a plan or a schedule, yet he always got where it felt like he was supposed to be, at just the right place and time. One of our last times together before he died, we were in line for coffee at Starbucks. We both ordered the Pike blend. That one was empty, so the barista offered us a few other options — *or* we could wait five minutes while more of the Pikes brewed. Being me, I jumped to the dark roast that was available immediately. Terry laughed and said, "Let's wait for the Pikes — it's all part of the ride." He was right. Our "agenda" for that sunny weekend day was to get coffee, walk around Hermosa Beach feeling the sun on our faces, people-watch, and just…"be." Waiting a few minutes more for the coffee we wanted was part of what the day was supposed to be about. It wasn't the warm-up, it *was* the ride.

One of my favorite quotes in *Fear and Loathing* is, "Buy the ticket, take the ride...and if it occasionally gets a little heavier than what you had in mind, well...maybe chalk it up to forced consciousness expansion: Tune in, freak out, get beaten."

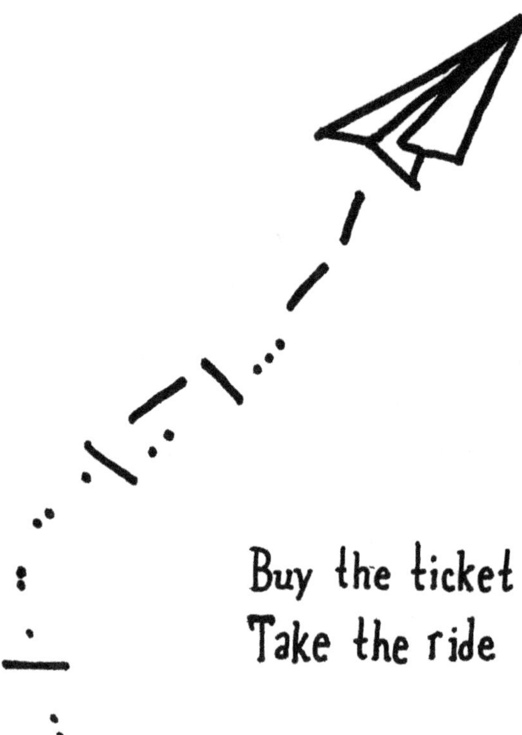

The ever-reliable Urban Dictionary explains "Buy the ticket/take the ride" as "creating and being involved in a situation that may get you in way over your head, but deciding that turning back would be a rather uninteresting option."

Tattooing this on my hand is my tribute to Terry, but most of all, it's another permanent reminder to myself to "take the ride" — *especially* when you don't know where it will let you off or what you will find waiting for you when it does. The unknowns, the journey, that's the source of most of life's true adventures. Adapting this philosophy in my personal life, especially as I built an unconventional family in a less formulaic way than most, as well as choosing a career path that has presented one adventure after another, is me buying the ticket — over and over again — and eagerly getting on the ride to 'who the fuck knows where.'

It's been a wild trip, for sure. I've negotiated with heavily armed tribal warriors in Ethiopia, dove head-first into Hollywood producing and directing, launched megabrands and sold enough stuff to make a lot of people rich, hit the kid jackpot (four times), started a wheelchair non-profit for people in developing countries… Launching a podcast was not the most impressive, most profitable, or most impactful. Not even close. But that doesn't mean it wasn't a significant stop on my journey.

By most people's standards, I've done a lot of living — the highest highs, along with rock-bottom lows that include loss and grief I will likely never fully come to terms with. So when everything came crashing down a couple of years ago, I knew that was not the end of the ride for me. It was the beginning of a new one. With no clear path ahead, I stepped back into my most natural comfort zone — being a storyteller, that recurring role I've been reimagining since I was a teenager — as my guide out of the darkness and my ticket to my next ride.

Having just turned 50, I'm stepping out yet again, embarking on another adventure — perhaps bigger and wilder than any prior. And I can't fucking wait.

CONCLUSION
PRESERVING MY HUMAN TATTOO MUSEUM

When I went on that life-changing tattoo journey in Bali, I came home with far more than I initially planned. Not only did I get a dope tattoo by a mega-talented artist and an unexpected, emotionally cathartic, tropical therapy session, but I also stumbled upon something else: I discovered my next act.

Less than twelve hours after finishing the elaborate, two-day-marathon chest tattoo, I decided to hike up Mount Batur volcano to watch the sunrise.

The hike starts well before dawn in pitch blackness, and ends, quite literally, up in the clouds, on top of a volcano — and weather and cloud-cover permitting, you witness an unrivaled sunrise.

Sounds fan-fuckin-tastic right? Well, because the hike starts around 3:45am, you freeze your balls off and layer up for warmth and protection from wind gusts. You are also reliant upon a small headlamp to guide you up unstable gravel, scattered with chunks of ashy lava rock while you huff and puff your way up to the peak. As the climb pushed on and it began to get lighter and warmer, I was becoming a sweat-soaked piece of human bacteria. I finally reached the top with a few minutes to spare before the highly-anticipated sunrise. And it was, hands down, the best sunrise of my life. The color and texture of the sky looked like something from an animated film.

And then the trippiest thing in my whole life happened: The photo taken of me at the top of the volcano mimicked the scene of the tattoo I'd just gotten with eerie accuracy — making it a sort of illustrated premonition, etched on my skin. Seriously fuckin' wild.

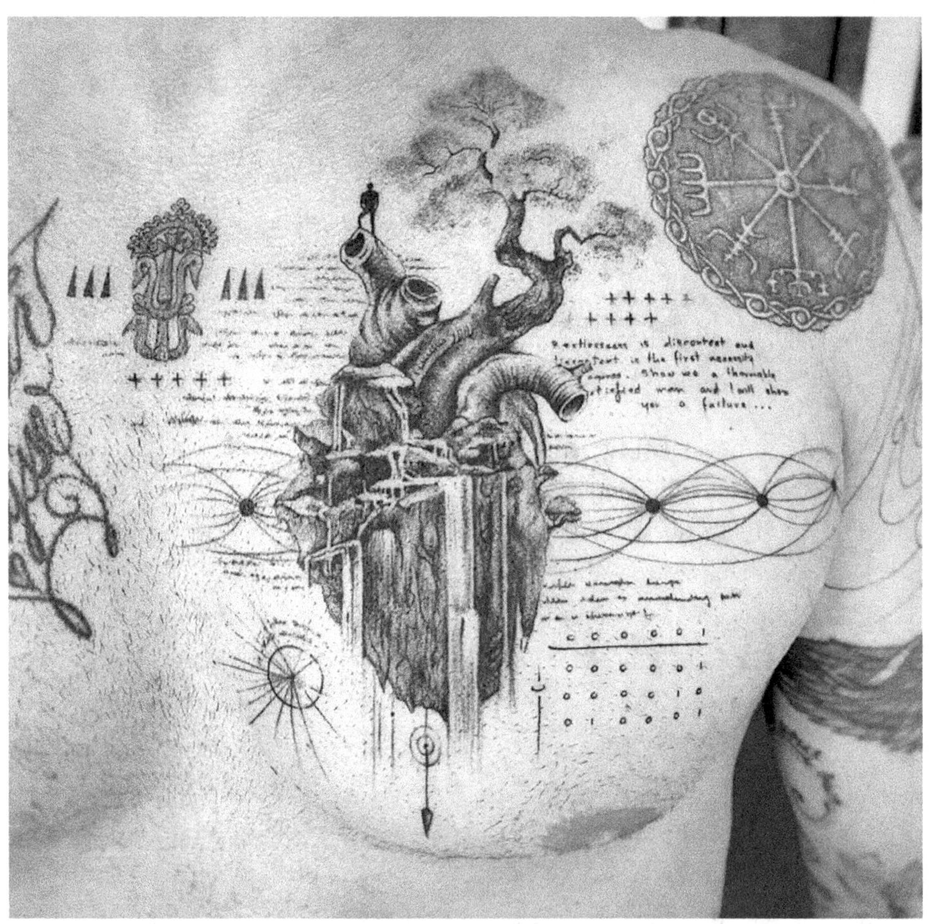

@balazsbercsenyi

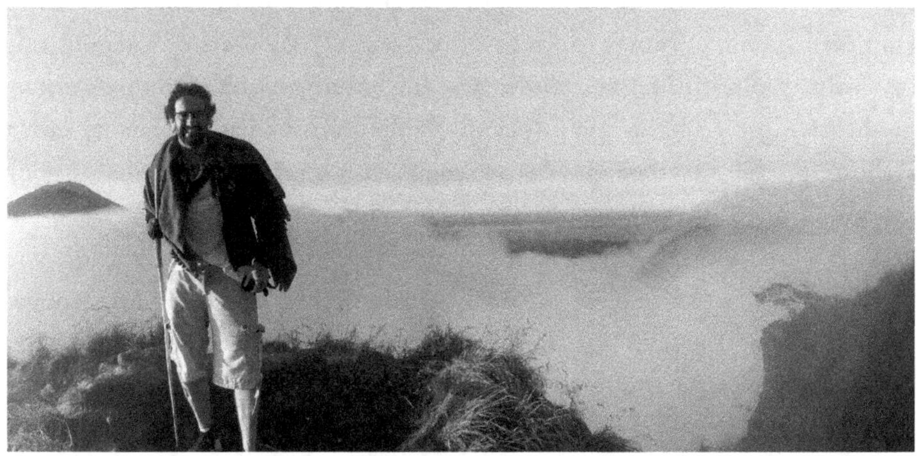
Sunrise atop Mt. Batur hours after new chest tattoo.

There was just one problem: As a result of the climb, my brand-new tattoo was drenched in sweat and coated with thick, volcanic ash (yeah, a major post-tattoo no-no). Even worse, I was flying back home in a few hours and had no way of treating and protecting the tattoo.

Itchy, scratchy, and fairly certain I'd soon see signs of an infection festering, I asked the driver taking me to the Bali airport to stop in the town of Ubud (which, coincidentally, roughly translates to "medicine"). Ubud is a mystical place and a mecca for seekers and healers, so fortunately there was no shortage of balms, aloes, and potions for sale.

I loaded up for my twenty-four-hour trip home, prepped to become my own guinea pig in this ill-advised dermatology experiment. (Warning kids: don't be an asshat like me and try this at home!) I mixed a bit of this with a dab of that mid-air, testing various concoctions. Whatever I (accidentally) did, it worked, because the itching stopped, the inflammation went down, and any would-be infection was avoided. The tattoo healed perfectly.

Upon returning to California, where I'd already spent fifteen years working with high-end skincare brands, I couldn't get that near-tattoo disaster out of my head. Surely I wasn't the only idiot who climbed a volcano with a fresh tattoo and raw skin? Ok, maybe I was… But I *definitely* wasn't the only person to nearly ruin a new tattoo after doing any number of irritating (and even moronic) things to my skin, post-tattoo. My years of accumulating detailed tattoo art made me wonder why there were no quality tattoo skincare products? Most people I knew, including tattoo artists, had no quality tattoo aftercare products at their disposal, usually settling for petroleum-based goop commonly used on a baby's ass for diaper rash or some faux "tattoo products" that are more concerned about profits than actual ingredients. More and more people were getting tattoos, many of which were incredibly detailed and vibrant. I knew I couldn't be alone in wanting to not only properly heal, but permanently preserve the spectacular works of art on my skin. Plus, for many of us, tattoos are more than art. They're symbolic, permanent markings of who we are. Caring for my tattoos means caring for everything my life's journey entails, preserved in my own personal human tattoo museum.

So I dove deeper into my science experiment and merged my professional experience with my personal passion to develop different, better tattoo skincare. Products that were made by real tattoo collectors like me for other tattoo collectors who wanted a tattoo aftercare option that did what it promised.

That's how Derm Dude™ was born.

I'd already spent years of my career working with renowned dermatologists and product formulators to help launch successful products for healthy skin and hair. But I never had real skin in the game (so to speak). Until now.

I reflected on the many professional stops I'd made up to that point: Writing and producing live TV news under the gun taught me to deliver ON TIME and with 100% accuracy. Plus, I learned to make quick, critical decisions when the pressure is on. Telemarketing is about as joyful as rapid-fire kicks to the balls. No one likes getting yelled at or hung up on. But those skills refined my mindset and approach to overcoming any and all objections and negativity while remaining hyper-focused and positive, even against all odds. And while people think there's a sexy, gritty glamor to bartending, in reality, you reach a certain age where you're hauling glassware upstairs at 2am and the fire and passion to forge a better path becomes far more appealing than free drinks with the bar staff. Producing numerous hit infomercials taught me to connect with real consumers by tapping into what really matters to them, with no scams, just real benefits and human story-telling. Plus, being a part of brands that sold over a billion dollars in products and services is not the worst confidence booster in the world when you decide to go all-in and launch your own brand from the ground-up.

My post-Bali venture — Derm Dude™ — a first-of-its-kind tattoo skincare and complete men's grooming line — allows me to now channel all of my life experiences at the right time. And as a kickass bonus, it allows me to finally establish my independence and create what I want on my terms, building a product-based lifestyle brand that reflects who I truly am.

And THAT had always been the question: *Who am I?* A Springsteen-obsessed Jersey kid? An imperfect product of an imperfect family? A failed journalist turned amateur podcaster? A successful L.A. agency owner and Hollywood director? A risk-taker who flopped as much as he soared? Yeah. All of that. And a million other labels and identities, the lessons from which I've spent a lifetime imprinting and journaling on my skin.

Each new tattoo is an invitation for reflection, but also for reinvention. An opportunity to shift and evolve who I am and what that means. Derm Dude™ is both my latest act and my source for physically preserving all the visible markers of my past and future reinventions: my tattoos. They're the reflection of what I was, as well as the promise of who I might become. They lay bare what's under my skin, by living so openly on its surface.

Tattoos are equal parts art, communication, and expression. But even, and perhaps especially, the truly shitty ones (*I'm looking at you, crying eyeball globe*) matter.

As my skin has evolved, so have I. The life I've captured and commemorated forms a cover that is certainly judged, even by me — but it's always evolving. And while we all may be critics, we can never truly understand or appreciate the significance of another person's tattoos: the associations they have with the imagery, the moment in time that prompted that permanent commitment. Some may consider themselves art collectors, but the true beauty of tattoos stems from the unspoken, the unwritten, the space between inked lines that only the person wearing it can fill in. It's their story to tell, their way. Our way.

Our skin is our body's largest organ. (Yeah, I know most guys believe otherwise but…)

And it does a LOT, like holding in all the other organs and keeping blood from oozing out all over. It also happens to be one badass canvas for communicating our thoughts, experiences and dreams. Our skin is alive, just as the stories we write on it are very much alive. Those stories live and breathe within our massive casing, our cellular sleeping bag, shielded from public view. For some, like me, those stories are also sprawled along the surface, a visual conversation piece with myself. Arguments, celebrations, pep talks, and negotiations alike.

Hundreds of thousands of puncture wounds are required for tattoos. Those tiny perforations, formed on my already porous skin, open the flow between the secret, private, internal stuff and the outside world. What was once invisible is transformed, needle by needle, into far more than collectible art. For me, the results of these puncture wounds fuel the most important conversations I ever have. Each tattoo might be a physical evolution or reinvention, but the transformation doesn't stop there. The moment the ink hits the flesh is just the beginning of the next chapter, a portal into a dialogue that is both recorded in permanent ink and forever retold and reinterpreted.

I've now entered my fifth decade, and for over half my life, I've been painting and plastering my internal dialogues on my skin. Each piece is additional food for thought: *Why did I get it? What does it teach me? Where am I falling short of what it's reminding me to do?* And while tattoos are hyper-personal, they also link us to the collective.

Some might think tattoos are modern and trendy. But in reality, evidence suggests humans have been tattooing themselves for millennia, all across the globe. One of the oldest tattooed bodies found, Ötzi the Iceman, dates back to around 3000 BCE. He had 61 tattoos. While the significance of the markings varied over time and across geographic regions, two things remained the same: They were permanent, and they hurt like a mother. And while advances in tattoo removal technology has sparked an increased interest in tattoos, the rite of passage that is the mind-numbing pain endures. The use of tribe-inspired symbols also carries over into modern society. Barbed wire or a teardrop from prisoner, a sailor's anchor, the samurai of the Yakuza — these markings are as much about cultural belonging now as they were thousands of years ago. A visual conversation that transcends time and language.

In *The Illustrated Man*, a collection of short stories written by Ray Bradbury, a washed up carnival worker is covered in tattoos, thanks to a mysterious traveling woman. Like all tattoos, each of the man's markings tells a different story. But unlike all tattoos, his ink moves at night and predicts the future. That's right: the illustrations come alive on his skin. Stung by magical needles, the man's tattoos foreshadow what's yet to come. Gazing at the man's body can foretell your own future. "They tell you a tale… It's all here, just waiting for you to look."

My body is not technically covered in magical ink, but for me, my tattoos *are* magical. The stories they tell are a living, breathing, perpetually evolving depiction of my life and the lives of those who've touched me.

All my life, I've wanted to be a storyteller. I thought my love of tattoos was separate from that childhood desire. But it turns out, they were the ultimate conduit. I wouldn't go so far as to call myself poetry in motion, but I am a giant, illustrated man whose body tells both short and, at times, painfully long stories: tragedies and comedies, happy endings and cliffhangers, horror stories and heart-warming tales. It's all right there, dancing imperfectly across the surface.

Look close enough, and you'll see what's *under my skin*.

APPENDIX

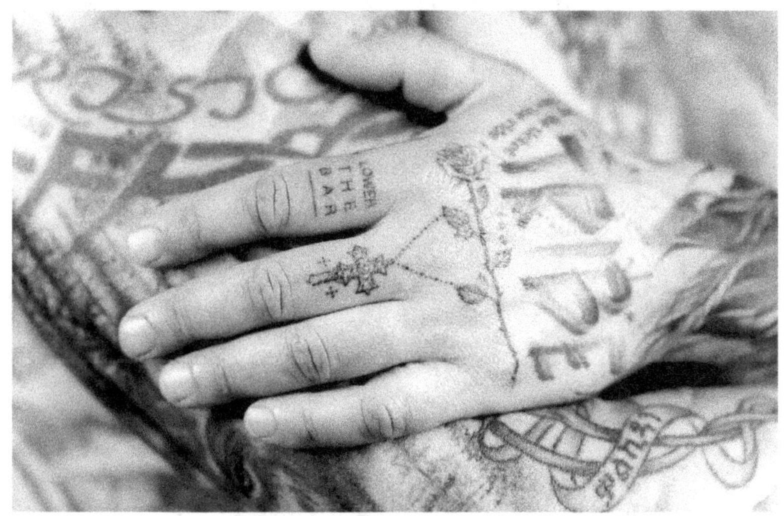

TRIBE: @georgiagreynyc   **Rose:** @mr.k_tattoo

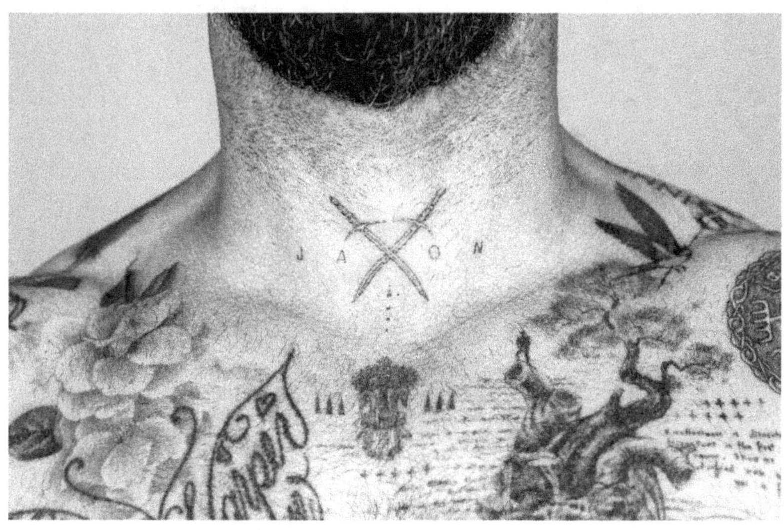

@mr.k_tattoo

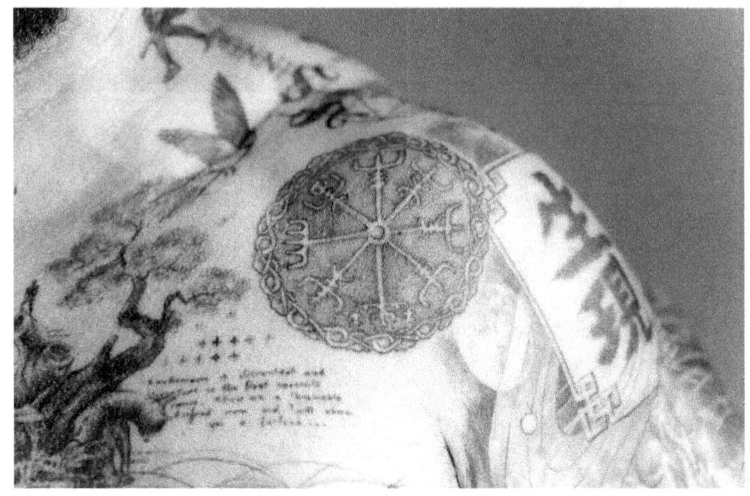

@rafael_valdez

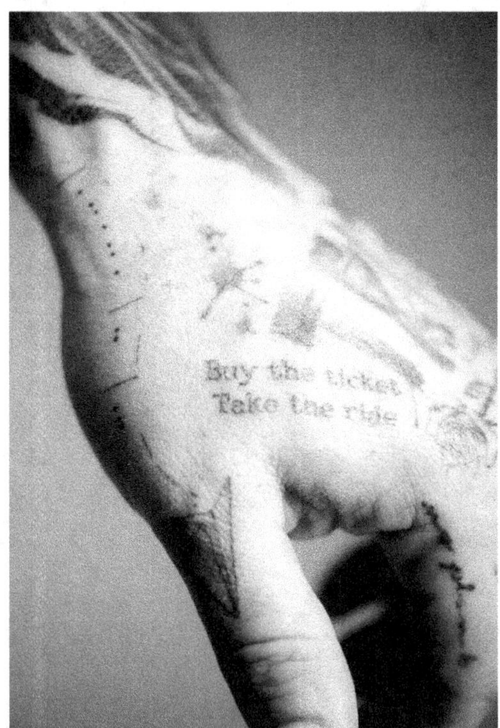

@sarahlotattoo

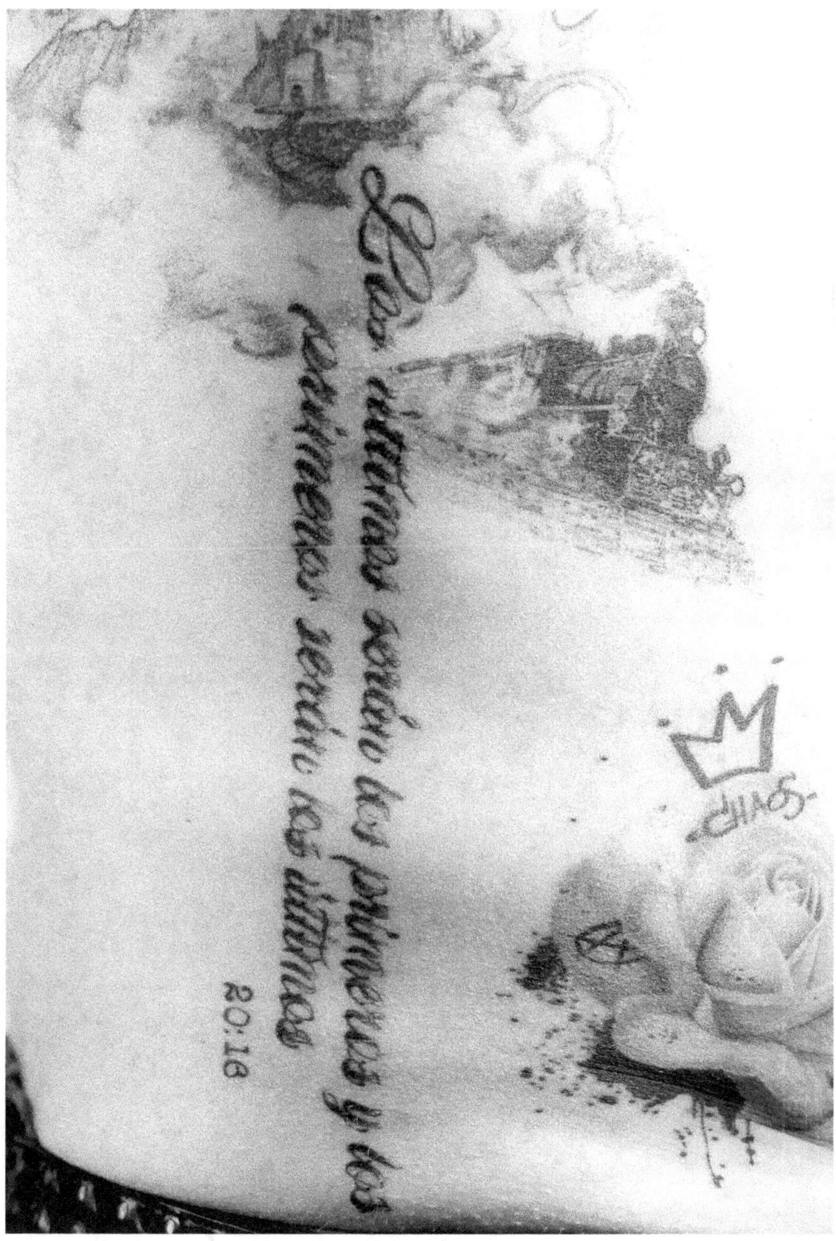

Train: @coldgraytattoo   **Rose:** @ponywave   **Proverb:** @vanda.tattoo

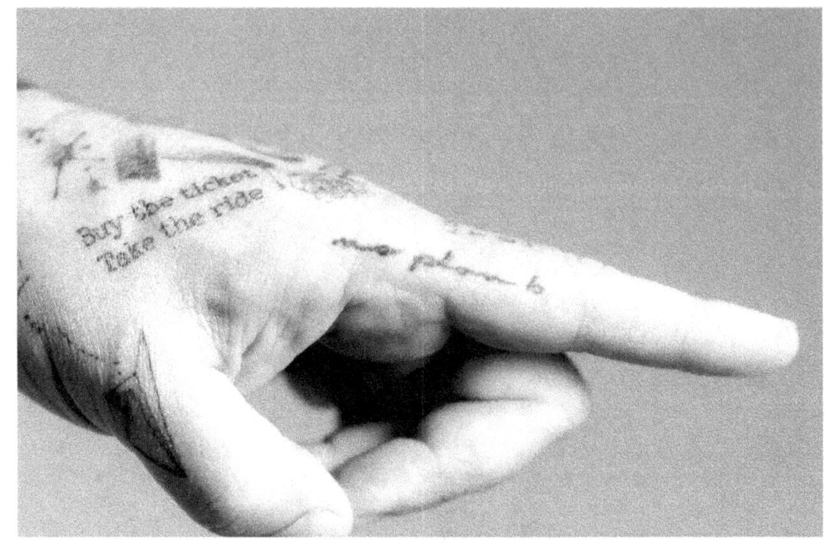

@jonboytattoo

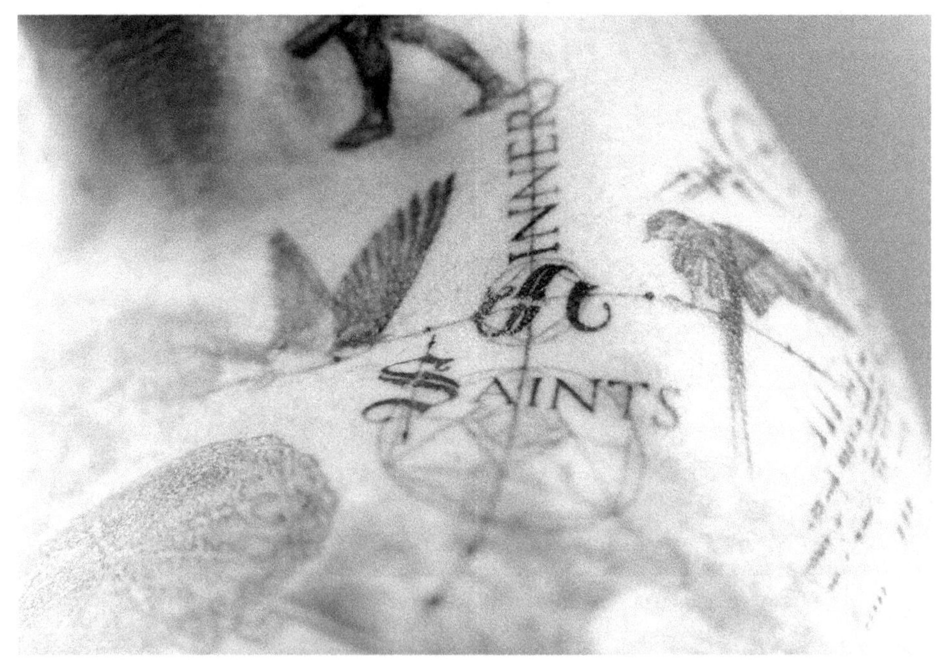

@oscarakermo

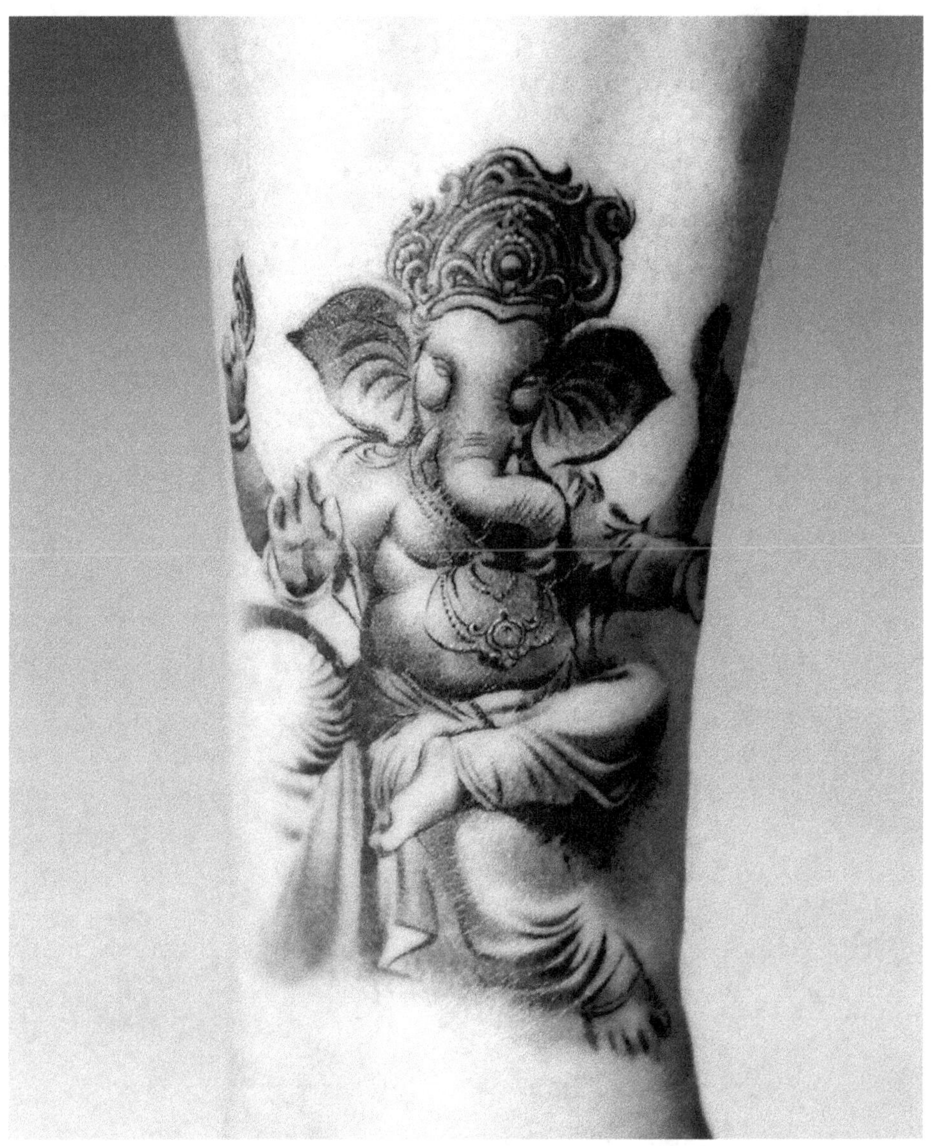

@vancurlytattoo

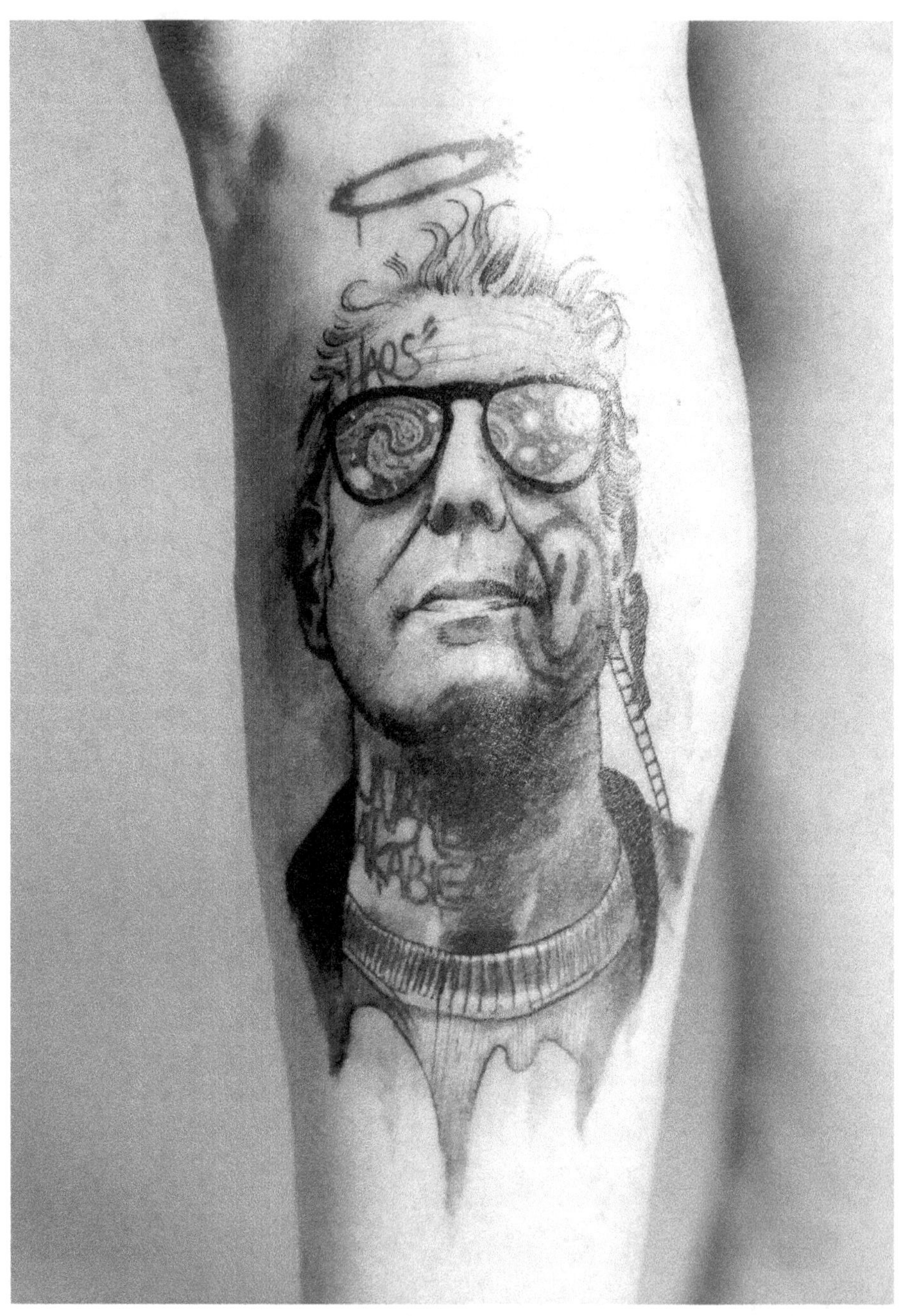

@kozo_tattoo

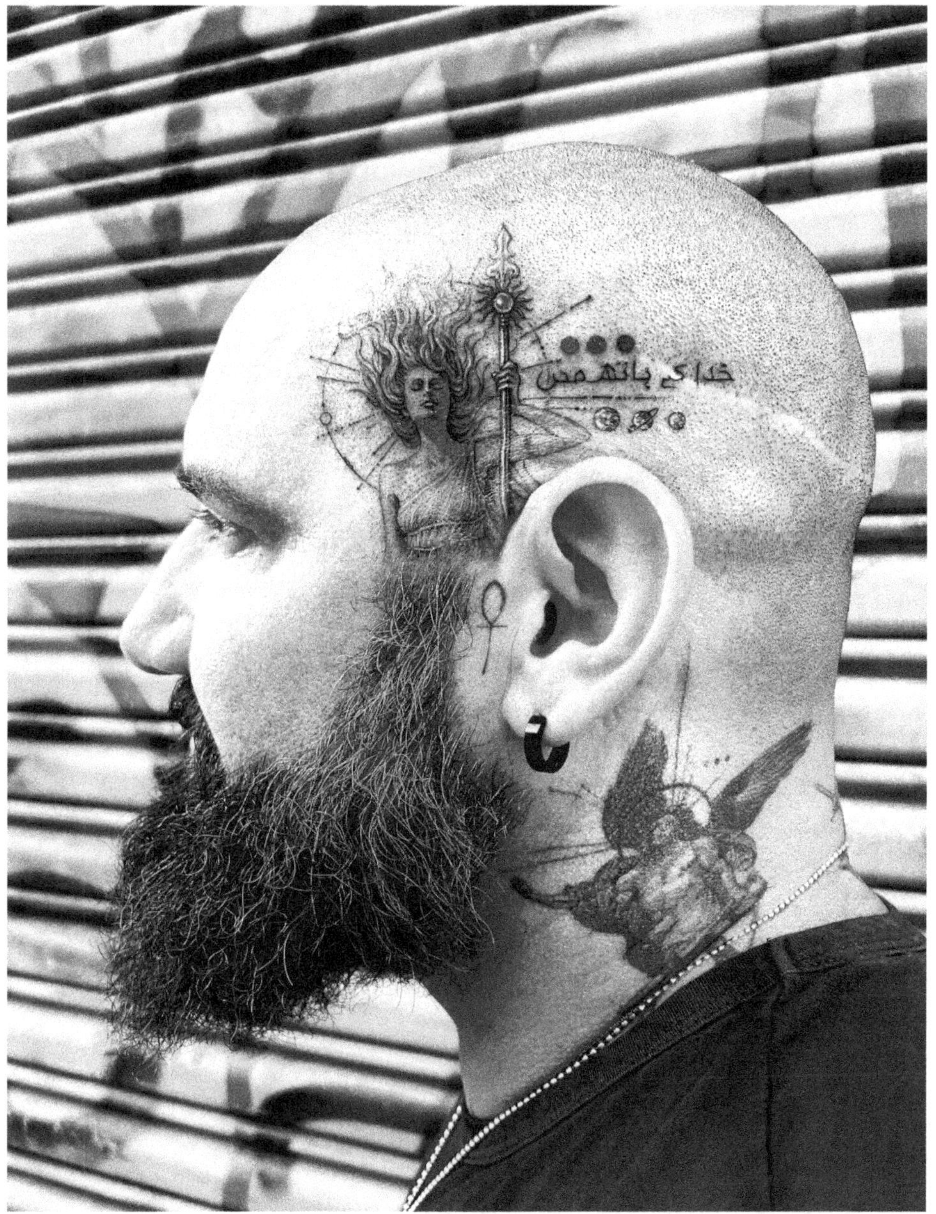

@mr.k_tattoo